THE WAY OF THE
EMPATH

THE WAY OF THE
EMPATH

How Compassion, Empathy, and Intuition Can Heal Your World

ELAINE CLAYTON

HAMPTON ROADS

Cover design by Kathryn Sky-Peck
Cover illustration by Artemenko Valentyn/Shutterstock
Interior photos/images by Elaine Clayton
Interior by Debby Dutton
Typeset in Adobe Caslon Pro, Kepler Std, and Raleway

Hampton Roads Publishing Company, Inc.
Charlottesville, VA 22906
Distributed by Red Wheel/Weiser, LLC
www.redwheelweiser.com

Sign up for our newsletter and special offers by going to
www.redwheelweiser.com/newsletter.

ISBN: 978-164297-037-1

Library of Congress Cataloging-in-Publication Data available upon
request.

Printed in the United States of America
IBI

10 9 8 7 6 5 4 3 2 1

For Dad

CONTENTS

INTRODUCTION:
THE ART OF
EMPATHY

Empathic sensing is the art of seeing the unseen and welcoming the mysteries of life through psychic events and fun encounters with yourself and others. Living as an empath means embracing the ideal of heart-centered intelligence by attuning to the experiences and well-being of others. Empaths seek to live a life of generosity through sensing and quiet knowing. This intuitive intelligence—this psychic clarity—is the hallmark of "knowing from the heart," the pinnacle of empathic knowledge.

An empath's life is not an ordinary life. It requires the strength of a lion, because it takes real courage to be empathic. This form of artful living asks that you develop your imagination, your curiosity, and your consciousness in an extraordinary way—that you discover how your perceptions guide and inform you, how they shape you and, at times, challenge you. It encourages you to step into your own innate role as creator and work to bring compassion and an open heart to yourself and others.

In this book, we will explore foundational principles of empathic living and psychic vision as a means to bring healing to the world. Here, we will discover ways to understand empathy, to embody mystical, spiritual, and imaginative insight through creative meditations and playful visualizations. Moreover, we will bring light to ways empaths must protect themselves while living with an open heart. This book offers some fundamental creative visualizations for that purpose as well.

I hope this book will open you to both great zeal and great mirth—the sign of true heart-centered intelligence—while helping you experience and appreciate synchronicity and serendipity. May it serve as a companion as you spin a brilliant heightened awareness full of wonderment and joy, depth of insight, and wild revelations.

> "I wish all the kind hearts would put their heads together!" (Julie Andrews, in the Broadway musical *Cinderella*)

CHAPTER 1
LIVING EMPATHICALLY

We are all sentient beings somewhere on an empathic spectrum, feeling our way toward deeper knowing and seeking, toward compassionate understanding and intuitive awareness. Some are born with an innate sensitivity to their surroundings and those in it—a proclivity that allows them to feel the presence of life energy in the atmosphere around both people and objects. Empaths sense the unseen, the energy that lies between and within the physical and material. Some develop empathic sensing through life experiences, perhaps by witnessing the suffering of a loved one or possibly through challenges like early childhood traumas that may spark ultra-sensitivity derived from emotional or physical danger. These experiences may cause some to be more compassionate because they have felt so much themselves and are able to see their own experiences reflected in the conditions of others.

This ability to feel what others feel—whether that be silent sorrows or overt expressions of pain derived from extraordinary circumstances—opens the door to a world of potential, of healing. A desire to cultivate a heightened sense of empathy and empathic awareness is a very spiritual and worthy undertaking, one that encourages the imaginal aspects of our creative natures to guide us to a balanced and meaningful life.

The duality of our existence means that we cannot avoid highs and lows in our lives. We all struggle as individuals to thrive despite the challenges we encounter. But we can learn to go through these experiences with a desire to feel them and an aspiration to understand them. With this understanding comes the potential for transformation and a sense of wonderment about the beauty in humanity. When we enhance our relationship with our higher selves by expanding our consciousness, rather than living lives in which we move from one reactionary episode to the next, we make room for deeper empathic connections with others. And we begin to create the life we'd most like to live. As empaths, our heart-centered intelligence helps us sense and understand what others feel as they grapple with their own life experiences, and this has a positive impact on all aspects of life.

> "I was always really sensitive. My two brothers were older than me and, when I was little, I cried easily if I thought someone was sad or hurt. But my brothers teased me for it."

Natural Empaths

Natural empaths are "sensitives" who have a genuine intuitive intelligence that allows them to feel the emotions of others as if those emotions were their own. Because they can easily sense the emotional "atmosphere" of a person or place, they are susceptible to the emotional, psychological, mental, and physical energy in the people and objects around them, and they must learn to cope with that. Some choose mystical paths and methods to help them cope, because they are generally open to sensing what is not visible—that is, energy. In fact, all natural empaths have an innate ability to sense spiritual energy, and to be accepting of it and oriented to it.

Empaths don't need practical proof of everything. They don't rely only on material or physical "reality" for knowledge and meaning. Thus empaths—whether their sensitivity is innate or acquired—live their lives as a quest for the spiritual and a desire for the transcendental. They seek to become mystically attuned, inspired, and healed. Moreover, they work to be a part of the healing of others, often pursuing professions in the healing arts. Because they are sensitive to the emotions of others, they often feel drawn to the unseen mysteries of life-force energy, and ardently seek to transform hardship through their quiet knowing. Empaths *feel* spiritual, they don't just think it; they are, literally, awe-inspired. Within their own physical being, from head to toe, they welcome spiritual allure. And that, in fact, is how empathy works, for the most part. Empaths *feel their way* through circumstances and relationships, and then mentally process what those feelings signify.

Life for empaths may seem less practical than for others, because, for them, the ordinary often gives way to elements of wonder, surprise encounters, emotional and spiritual connections, and a sense of mystery. The unseen forces of emotional and mental energy tend to dominate empaths' lives, because they are always on the lookout for moments of gentle appreciation, for spontaneous spiritual connections, and for compassionate exchanges with others. They are always open to elucidations of what, to others, seems ordinary.

Because empaths carry within them an inclination to love unconditionally, it is important to understand that there is no love without self-love. Those who lack self-compassion or patience or self-forgiveness cannot reflect authentic strength in fellow feeling.

Self-love is the starting point of empathy. Empaths feel love easily; they see beyond the personalities of others and connect instead with their soul essence. But without self-love, self-respect, and self-forgiveness, they may find themselves bereft, exhausted, or feeling worthless; they may end up in a struggle with the self-loathing facet of the ego that dominates the thinking mind. They may even be worn down to the point that they excuse the actions and choices of others. They may ignore warning signs and pretend not to notice when something does not feel right.

Encompassing another's soul essence is a beautiful feeling. But empaths must also learn to be direct and honest with themselves when blending with others in relationships. Ultimately, developing discernment without self-punishment is crucial, as is practicing self-love and self-forgiveness.

Empathic Impressions

The mental processing of intuitive-empathic impressions usually occurs *after* the initial gathering of emotive energy rather than in the moment. Through repeated experience, empaths develop a response mechanism that envelops on-the-spot compassion and combines it with kindly self-containment. They learn not to be so influenced by the hurt or even the agendas of others that they get swallowed up or swept away by them. Because they are sensitive, they are susceptible. When empaths are moved by the words or experiences of others—when they react immediately with mercurial feelings of empathy—they can easily lose themselves in the exchange and make themselves vulnerable. The feelings of others can become theirs and be felt within their own physical being.

> "If I go to a party, everyone's energy slams me. I feel this person's tension and that person's anger and that person's wish to forget pain. I can tell when someone is holding back and I easily get uncomfortable. I start feeling all this and, before I know it, it's as if they're my own emotions. Yet, when I arrived, I was feeling fine."

That is why it is often beneficial for empaths to review their own emotions and impressions after a conversation or encounter and to sift through why they feel the way they do. Perhaps they received so many impressions that they could not mentally process them all in the moment. Or perhaps they need to ask themselves what actually happened in a given encounter and how that experience made them feel. Empaths are caught in a daily storm of varying emotive sensations, even in the most casual of exchanges with others. For them, events that anyone else may consider meaningless and forgettable may seem significant. Reflecting on these empathic storms, in which they are inundated with the emotions or thoughts of others, can help them cope with the residual feelings that may surface for them once the interactions have ended and the cloudburst has subsided.

This time of reflection helps empaths review their impressions and find their own place for centering again. It helps them to clarify for themselves what they felt during an encounter and try to understand why they felt it. This takes time, but it is time well spent, because it keeps empaths from getting layered with residual emotions to the point of breaking down. When empaths do end up immersed in the energy of others, whether they want it to happen or not, they must then deal with the consequences.

Pivotal Awareness

When empaths feel a barrage of details coming at them in the form of feelings, impressions, and realizations, they deal with them as best they can in the moment. But there is no internal peace for them until those feelings are processed and acknowledged. This happens several times a day for most empaths, usually with every encounter and in every physical space they enter. Once they develop pivotal awareness that allows them to empathize without taking on responsibility for the pain or predicament of others, however, they can more easily manage these emotional onslaughts. By becoming conscious of what is happening *while it is happening*, and acknowledging that they don't have to soak it all up in the moment, they realize that the woes they are encountering belong to others and not to themselves. This makes them stronger spiritually, and enables them to be strong for others as well, offering care and listening without being inundated energetically. Instead of drowning in the downpour of impressions, they become able to connect with others through heart-centered healing energy and prayers for their well-being.

> "When I was a teenager, my mother told me every time I spent time with this one friend, I came home in a terrible mood. I realized I was juggling all of the feelings and energy of that person and that a lot of it was negative. It was going directly from her into me. Sometimes I'd have anxiety from so much energy coming at me. I had to get away from that."

It is not an empath's job to rescue anyone, although most empaths have tried—and perhaps many times over. Although they may feel crushed by what others have suffered, it is simply not their responsibility to be "fixers." This does not mean that empaths don't take meaningful action when they can; they often take part in efforts and initiatives to advocate for others. But empaths are at their best when they realize they are not the grand overseers of others' lives. Nor are they the personal *consiglieri* of others, although they may very much wish they could help heal those they care about, even those who may try to draw them into every personal drama. Most empaths learn—sometimes the hard way—that they cannot manage or heal any adult life other than their own. Once they discover ways to take ethical action using their empathic skills without getting enmeshed in the sagas of others, they become more stable and are able to enjoy the many wonderful aspects of being empathic.

Synchronistic events, signs, and mysteriously interesting happenings are what empaths live by and for, even when doing everyday tasks. For empaths, that which is material, physical, or concretely fixed is not just solid mass, because even inanimate objects carry some kind of energetic vibration. Empaths get a surge of energy from *everything*. For them, objects give off a frequency and a quality of personality that is deeply felt and cannot be ignored. They often attribute human qualities to objects, playfully "seeing into" or even "seeing through" whatever they encounter at any given time. They also know when something feels "good" and when it gives off an unpleasant vibe. In fact, they are spiritually psychogenic toward objects they handle or use. But how do these impressions arise?

> "I wanted to enjoy browsing in the antique shop, but found myself in a soup of disturbing feelings, as if I sensed all these people who had lived and died. There were heavy sentiments attached to the antiques. I had an overwhelming feeling about each thing I laid my eyes on, not to mention when

I touched things. It wasn't that this was negative energy, but it was all just too much to take in. A silver sable brush or some old oval mirror, a tool chest made of oak—all the objects in the place just weighed me down inside. It was as if I felt the lives of all the people who had used those things and I had to get out and breathe fresh air."

Empathic Sensing

Empaths receive what may not be visible or immediately obvious to others through a "sixth sense"—the mind's eye, or third-eye visions. They pick up on this wave of feeling, which is often sensed as psychic imagery, internalizing it all and projecting their perceptions back outward. In fact, they "see" in ways that are quite like the way we see when we dream, when our physical eyes are closed. Empaths may receive input from this sixth sense all day long—seeing

color, details of rooms or spaces, features of landscapes or places, and all kinds of people and animals. These third-eye visions are at times like seeing "through a glass darkly," and at times as clear as if seen in broad daylight.

Although empaths may appear to be focusing on events or circumstances in the moment, such as in group conversations, they may also be inwardly seeing what is unfolding on a completely different level on a screen in their minds. They may be listening, but also sensing strongly what is left unsaid, what is felt beneath the surface of people around them. They may be watching the aura of light around others or picking up on some inward sadness that goes unnoticed or appears irrelevant to most. Empaths continually see these mental images—these flashes of colorful and impressive visions—as information streams in their minds that enter through the third eye or in other forms.

This kind of seeing and sensing, without the use of the physical eyes, is most common during the dream state, in which scenes arrive and change in a multi-dimensional or multi-faceted way. In fact, paying attention to dreams is one way we can develop empathic knowing. Many people don't recall their dreams, however, or the emotions that accompany them. A lot of content in our dreams gets lost when we wake up and quickly get busy with the routines of the day. We tend to switch out of the stream of consciousness that dominates our dreams once we are awake. But when we learn to harness this powerful way of perceiving—when we don't switch it off too quickly upon waking—it can be a life-changer.

Empaths often speak of *not being able* to switch off their multitudinous and often overwhelming dreams. They describe cinematic scenes that leave strong impressions and very emotive themes that won't let go of them. They sometimes cannot shake these dreams once awake and their dreams often follow them throughout the day, as if plastered on their foreheads right in front of the third eye. Basically, empaths live in something like a perpetual dream state. Even while they are awake and focused on their responsibilities, a lot of other extra-sensory information is moving through them, coming at them, and lingering with them.

> "When my dreams stay with me during the day, it is usually because there is a central character that is magnetic. It may be a person or it may be something like an animal or a tornado, but it is a focal point. And if I am able to put the dream aside, I revisit it until I think I understand why I had it."

Sometimes using the empathic third eye during the day leaves empaths waiting a while to validate that their inner feelings are correct. Since they are sensing what others may not, they may feel alone in their efforts to understand what they receive in the way of hunches and gut reactions. Empaths often act as the Cassandras of the office or family, voicing what they see much to the chagrin of others who don't see the same things—or don't see them *yet*.

> "I didn't feel right about someone I worked with, although everyone else said she was a great person. I had a feeling of distrust around her, however, so I kept my distance at the office. It turned out that she was stealing things from the domestic violence shelter and eventually got caught."

Deep sensing guides empaths if they pay attention to the prominence of the impressions delivered. It has a grounding as well as an uplifting positivity for them, even if they have to bear the brunt of being the one who says: "I told you so." Having this extra sight gives empaths a mass of information to sift through, and this can help them navigate all kinds of situations or ordeals—and even create solutions to practical everyday problems. But the sheer amount of information they must process can lead to overload as well. Most of what we are expected to do from a young age is to react appropriately to external inputs—listen to the teacher; clear the table; play the game; study for the test. We are rarely encouraged to turn inward, to listen to intuitive, heartfelt messages from inside ourselves.

Young Empaths

Education is a privilege and there's a lot to be said for "getting with the program." Yet empathic children must try to fulfill the expectations of others and of the system while being hyper-aware of a lot of unspoken, but strongly felt, impressions—for instance, the emotional energy of teachers, parents, or peers, or perhaps their thoughts or underlying agendas. They are continually sensing the fluctuating energetic atmosphere around people and within their surroundings. They may be seeing what is really going on, or intuiting what the emotional implications of a situation are, or perceiving dynamics that others ignore or may not even recognize. Very young empaths may not have the verbal skills to describe what they are experiencing or may blurt out what others won't say or don't wish to acknowledge. Young empaths often go through their entire childhood dealing with overload, keeping up with demands while having to focus on a lot of intuitive content in the form of thoughts and feelings.

> "In school, I'd think of a word, and all of the sudden the teacher would say it. I don't know why; it would just happen. And it might be a word not commonly used and this would happen several times a day."

Young empaths may not concentrate enough on a proposed agenda or the assignments given to them, because they are inwardly doing much more than that. They may be accused of not "paying attention" or not "working hard enough," or told they are wasting time daydreaming. Thus empathic sensing can shape children's self-perception because it may make them feel somewhat alienated from others or not a part of the social scenes they observe. They may be described as having "fallen behind," or they may not be rewarded as often as their peers because they seem to wander or speak of what they see in ways that rub others the wrong way. Yet trying to stop empaths from sensing empathically is simply not possible. It is like asking them to unsee what they have seen or deny what they know. But empathic intelligence is a compelling force; denying it does no good. Moreover, empathic sensing is entertaining; it is centered in creativity and originality. At times, it has a presentient quality.

> "In the dream, this person at school approached me and asked me if I wanted a pair of pants she had bought that didn't fit her. That morning at school, this same person walked up to me and

told me she had pants for me that she thought would fit me better than they fit her. And she gave them to me on the spot, just like in the dream."

Quiet Knowing

Empathic sensing is seated in quiet knowing that comes without effort. This quiet knowing guides empaths to register what is not immediately or superficially obvious. And this can sometimes get interesting. The facades and surface presentations that drive social or professional interactions can be funny at times. But empaths sense what is going on *beneath* those surface exchanges. They look beyond surface impressions because the energy beneath or within the actions, words, or visual input is too evident to them, and this can sometimes make everything seem like a charade. In fact, this may be one way in which we all experience empathic impressions. We all frequently see through the actions and behaviors of ourselves and others. This is how we live and learn and become more capable of discerning with more judgment and integrity.

When empaths suppress the sensations of quiet knowing that they feel in any given encounter or situation, they live to regret it, because they *know* they knew what they knew but denied it. By so doing, they lose the opportunity to process the knowing.

We've all felt nervous when meeting a charming and kindly person or entering a spectacular and lovely space, and yet felt negative vibes. And we all know what it feels like when we ignore those warning signs—that something other than that which meets the eye is present. We end up saying something like: "I *knew* I should have avoided that person/place/thing." Or: "I knew it; I felt it. But I didn't listen to myself."

Learning these lessons the hard way is part of the initiation process for empaths. In fact, since all of us are somewhere on the spectrum of empathic sensing, and since all empaths are empaths in training, we are all, in one way or another, learning through experience using logical reasoning as well as intuition. We are all developing consciousness and insight as we live and breathe. No matter where we are on the journey to honor compassionate sensing and mystical guidance, we know when we have paid attention to the signs and messages of empathic intelligence—and when we have ignored them. That is how we learn. The more we tune in to the messages mysteriously given and received, the more we honor our intuitive knowing, the more exciting and rewarding our lives become.

Sensing what is felt in others and caring empathically about it is, in many ways, the fiber that connects us to one another in our humanity. However, the professional roles people play—for example, roles in which they may *not* be given to seeing beneath surface projections or may *never* feel inundated with the emotions of others—are valuable as well. People get amazing things done and can benefit others greatly without necessarily having an empathic orientation to life. They may be doers-of-great-things and movers-of-mountains; they may be scientists or technical geniuses. They may never immerse themselves in empathic sensing, or they may not come to it until later in their lives. But the world is in need of all kinds of talents, actions, and improvements. And we all have unique gifts and skills that have their own value.

Yet it is fair to say that, without empathy and compassion—or even a fruitful curiosity about how others feel—a lot of damage can be done. Some level of empathic sensing is necessary in all human relations and activities, because we are all so greatly impacted by one another, by the structures within which we operate, and by our surroundings and environment.

CHAPTER 2

DREAMS, SIGNS, AND SYNCHRONICITIES

Empaths are dreamers and daydreamers. They notice signs and synchronistic happenings that may originate while they sleep or that play out during the day. They commonly go through their waking hours in something like a dream state; during their sleeping hours, quite lucid information may stream in. And this is really exciting.

Seeking wisdom through dreams, signs, and synchronicities is really fun because, when you are open to the expectation and anticipation of these events, you are delighted when you recognize them happening. So much is possible once you develop a strong companionship with your imaginative subconscious self. Often, the line between sleep and wakefulness blurs and you begin to see elements from inside a dream during the day—sometimes unexpectedly. Empaths often remark on how exhilarating this can feel when it happens.

Some signs that empaths say they notice regularly include:

- *Cardinals.* "It is my grandmother saying hello."

- *Coins.* "I found one in the shower as if it came out of nowhere!"

- *Feathers.* "I heard an owl outside my window. In my mind, I asked it for one of its feathers. The next day, while walking the dog in the backyard, I found a huge owl feather beside a tree."

- *Repeating numbers* (3:33, 11:11, 2:22, etc.). "Every time I look at a clock, it's 3:33!"

"After my mother died and I returned from her funeral, I got into an argument with my spouse and, just as we were pretty much shouting at each other on the outside steps, a feather drifted down from an open sky. No trees above! It floated first to my husband's nose as if to tickle it, then it drifted down and landed at my feet. It was small and red. My mother had red hair. I knew it was a sign from her; I felt her presence and our disagreement ended right there."

As you learn to appreciate signs and synchronicities, keep your journal by your side. Write down in an intuitive discourse *why* you want to receive signs and experience synchronicities through dreams and during the day. Perhaps you want psychic-intuitive knowing in your dreams and signs the next day that can validate the psychic messages. Write it all down as a signal to the universe, to the Source of Life, that you are actively participating in spiritual knowing.

Dreams and Daydreams

Dreams and astral travel—being consciously aware of "going places" out of the body while either asleep or awake—can be the source of highly beneficial empathic impressions. And since what is experienced in dreams can unveil all kinds information, this can be fascinating content to explore. Empaths know that third-eye visions open portals to intuitive, quiet knowing, to realizations, and to revelations.

The lessons learned through hardships exhibited in the dream state (as if they "really happened") can guide the heart and spirit that feels them through the mire of human conditions experienced in the waking state. Sometimes these lessons can even serve as warnings or clues or tip-offs. Who has not had a terrible dream and awoken to exclaim: "I'm so glad that was only a dream!" Dreams show us what we want to avoid. And some show us what we most long for as well. When dreams arrive, dreamers experience a range of emotions; they get ideas and clearer insights, and often wake up feeling renewed. In fact, to ignore all that is offered in the dreamtime (day or night) is detrimental to empaths, since dreaming and daydreaming contain truths and lessons by which they learn and grow.

As an empath, there are several simple things you can do to deepen your dreaming as a way to empathic knowing. They include journaling, using affirmations, cultivating your imagination, creating intuitive play, and aligning with your ideals. Let's look at each, one by one.

Journal Your Dreams

Establishing a good rapport with the self that sleeps and dreams—with the spiritual self, the astral self, the poetic self—is one of the greatest gifts an empath can have. This is easy to do, even if you don't usually remember your dreams. In fact, developing the ability to remember your dreams is an intuitive skill that can be highly transformative.

If you want to receive intuitive knowledge from your dreams, but do not usually remember them, start by saying aloud every day (or even several times a day): "I *will* remember my dreams tonight. I *will* remember my dreams tonight." Keep a journal by your bedside in case you wake up. If you wake up and a dream is still fresh in your mind, try not to move so as not to lose the dream feeling and vision. Write down (without looking, if you can) a few notes or words about the dream, enough so that, in the morning, you will recognize what it was about from just the briefest of descriptions.

Drinking water before bed may help you to wake up in the night so you can jot down dream imagery or emotions.

Within about two weeks of this disciplined effort, you will start to remember your dreams, or at least some of them. Once you do, journal those dreams and really spend time capturing the *feelings* within the dreams, contemplating their impact and meaning for you.

Use Affirmations

We all daydream and at times even dream about what we want most in life. Daydreaming opens us to imaginal transcendence. And you can use affirmations to ask that what you wish for can come true. Affirmations have great power as visually impactful statements of your own self-assertion and ingenuity. When you concentrate on your ardent wishes and picture them coming true, you validate your ability to assert that which you'd most like to experience. The thoughts you generate when you revel in your daydreams stirs your consciousness and encourages you to align with your wishes. Sometimes, you don't even want to wake up from them.

Affirmations represent a kind of magical thinking, because they indicate that we have the will and power and determination to experience or manifest our specific desires. Affirmations can be verbal (spoken or sung aloud) or tactile, especially when they are written down and we actually feel the sensation of writing. Some affirmations consist of physical gestures made while daydreaming, like drawing, or painting, or sewing, or even taking a walk or dribbling a basketball. Having a way to signal what we wish to experience is essential, because, as human beings, we are creators and manifestors. This is who we really are; we can make things happen.

We are often shy about asking for what we want because we fear we won't get it. Or perhaps we hesitate to open our hearts and express our personal likes and dislikes, our yearnings and hopes. And in fact, it is easy to feel disappointed or vulnerable ("I'll never get what I want, so why don't I just forget it altogether?") and to hide what we most desire even from ourselves. But whether or not you feel you deserve to have your wishes fulfilled or believe that it will ever happen, training yourself to declare what you most want is essential. It is the bedrock on which you can build a life that is aligned with your deepest desires—a life in which you see yourself as a creator.

To engage in empathic affirmations, you must *feel* the desired outcome from head to toe. You must align with the energy of how you imagine it would feel if you had already realized that outcome. Feel it as if it already *is*. Don't make a pity list of things you always wanted but know you will never have. This is just a waste of time that will leave you frustrated and upset. Focus on the things about life that you admire, value, and love. Affirm to yourself that you are a unique individual with specific preferences.

You can give your affirmations added force by writing them down or saying them out loud with a feeling of appreciation for them. Consider that you already have the things you want on a cosmic level, because you can feel the energy in them. For example, if, more than anything, you want a life that includes riding horses, don't think about that desire in a negative way: "I love horses, so why don't I have one?" Instead, take a walk and dedicate it with a positive affirmation like: "I dedicate this walk to my love of horses and wish to have my own. To have my own horse that I can ride every day would feel so exciting. I love how horses smell, how much fun it is to groom them. I'd groom mine all the time. I love saddling up a horse, and the smell of the leather. I love how it feels to trot through the woods and canter across an open field, the wind in my hair." This makes the entire walk an affirmation of love, not of disappointment. It brings you into vibrational alignment with your wish and makes it "yours" simply because you are stating your love of what you desire.

> "I met a corporate psychic at a party in Seattle. I sat and talked with her for a bit. She said that her mother told her: 'If you love it, it's yours.' Then she told me that all that I loved was already mine and that I should try not to feel as if I didn't have what I wanted. She said that what you want comes to you when you love it, because you love it. Sooner or later. I never forgot that."

Cultivate Imagination

The imagination is very important as a spiritual conduit and as a creator of human connection and fulfillment. Our imaginations seem to create a momentum that puts our wishes into action on the material plane. The inifinite dimensions of possibility invoked by our imaginations help create an intuitive structure, like building an ethereal castle in the air that ultimately engages with the physical world. In fact, the imagination *is where it all happens!* All good things exist in our minds as ideas first, before we help manifest them on this plane of existence. Cultivating our imaginations is integral to living creative lives and fundamental to living an empathic life.

One way to cultivate your imagination is to create an entire wall upon which you can write out your dreams—a kind of expanded dream journal dedicated to your imaginative wanderings and your ideas and thoughts. If you can dedicate an entire wall to this, you will be able to watch your imagination taking form. If you can, paint the wall with chalkboard paint, which comes in lots of different colors, so you can change it whenever you like, using chalk to jot down your ideas or draw your impressions. If you cannot use an entire wall, tape large pieces of paper to a wall instead and use them to record your imaginative thoughts. If that isn't possible either, you can always use a notebook and a pen or pencil to create a treasured book of imaginal transformation.

The imagination is very active and worth nurturing. In your imagination, just about anything goes. Don't be afraid to commit your thoughts, ideas, and wishes, your feelings and impressions, to paper or to a larger wall surface to foster your imagination and help it grow.

> "I needed a new saddle, but could not afford it. A friend told me to visualize a new saddle. I said: 'Oh, like a saddle is gonna just fall out of the sky?' And she said very seriously: 'Yes.' A few days later, I saw on E-bay that a woman in Germany needed a saddle like mine. And I wanted one like hers. So we traded saddles and it did not cost either of us a penny."

Create Intuitive Play

Empaths feel more centered when their imaginations thrive and when they create in ways that bring them joy. Being playful is one way to keep these channels open to receive empathic knowing. When we allow our creative expression to be playful and intuitive, invention and solutions follow.

If you are not sure what creative activity would make you happy, start by making simple collages. Rather than choosing a complicated project that stresses you out or some activity that does not lift your spirits, just let yourself get lost in the daydream of your beautiful creative spirit by collaging imagery you love to look at. Find images in magazines that really appeal to you and cut them out and paste them on a poster board or an old shoebox. Carefully chosen visual imagery helps you align with what you love about living and that stimulates creativity and aligns you with your ideals. All you need to do this is a pair of scissors, some glue, old magazines filled with images that please you, and some poster board or a cardboard box.

Align with Your Ideals

What each of us loves is unique because *we* are unique. Edgar Cayce, the 20th-century mystic known as the Sleeping Prophet, offered great wisdom on what it means to be true to our own uniqueness and thereby appreciate the uniqueness of others. Cayce entered trance states and gave readings that included previously unknown (but now commonly used) healing methods and spiritual guidance. In one reading, he stressed the importance of holding fast to our ideals: "Each individual entity, whether aware of same or not, sets before self an ideal in the material world, in the mental world, in the spiritual world" (*Reading 1011-1,* Association of Research and Enlightenment Archives).

Our ideals shape how we live and how we make choices. Even if we do not see them reflected in the world, we still hold them and can align with them by becoming more conscious of exactly what they are so we can bring them about in our experience. What we prize most in love relationships, in society, in nature, in the essence of time and our presence on earth *matters.* Thus becoming conscious of our ideals is fundamental to living an empathically attuned life, because, without this awareness, we do not know what motivates us or why we have certain impulses.

To welcome this conscious awareness of your ideals, it helps to write them down. Create a mental landscape where you can experience what you love through your imagination. That alone will influence actions and choices that may bring you what you love.

When you spend time reflecting on what you love, what you hold as personal ideals, you open your soul. Think of your ideals as your soul itself or the quality of your soul as it lives through your humanity. To be empathic is, in essence, to be aligned with love, with what you love, and with knowing what you love. Your ideals can change through time, and choices you make can reflect that. But spending time remembering your ideals will make your empathic spirit sing. As Miggs Burroughs, artist, designer, and author of *What If?* (2012) wrote when asked about his own ideals:

> If I had a magic wand, I would give the standard Miss America answer of wanting to wipe out hunger, poverty, and hate. But more realistically, one of my highest ideals is to get through each day with more compassion for "the other guy." What would the world look like if we could all adopt that simple agenda? Maybe it actually could put an end to hunger, poverty, and hate. What if?

When considering how you would identify your own highest ideals, ask yourself:

- What are the virtues I hold dearest?
- What would the best kind of romantic relationship look like?
- What makes a good friend?
- What makes a true political leader?
- How do I think children should be treated?
- What is the job I'd love most?
- To what location do I feel most attracted?

Dwell on what you love about this life. Feel it; sense it. Know that it is real right inside of you and that you can create it from within and then outwardly realize it. If you are not conscious of what you love, you won't recognize it when it comes your way.

Synchronistic Signs

Empaths live in a powerful state of receiving that which seems almost impossible to others. They are open to receiving as a way of life. This means that they expect to receive signs and fully accept the notion that we truly do receive what is needed and often what is wanted, simply through being open and aware.

> "I was driving home from an errand thinking I wanted to go to the museum the next day. Then I realized the museum was closed on Mondays in the summer. When I got home, I took the dog out for a walk and encountered another woman out walking. We said hello and I asked her how her summer was going. She replied: 'More hectic than usual.' When I asked why, she told me that she worked at the museum and that they were open on Mondays in the summer, so she had to work more often. I was amazed that my inward wish to go to the museum on a Monday was fulfilled by a chance meeting with a stranger."

Asking for signs is very empowering for empaths, because they almost always receive them. When they wake up and have intuitive spiritual conversations, or set intentions for the day by asking for help, or ask to receive guidance, this literally creates the kind of reality they desire.

They are confident that signs will be given and answers will arise. And because these signs usually arrive in their own time, empaths live a life of pleasant surprises. Cultivating expectation and resisting the urge to be disappointed is a disposition that empaths recognize as being most beneficial.

> "I dreamed the hard things I was going through were like designs on a spiritual robe that showed what I had been through and that I had healed. I wanted to believe that meant that the misery I felt would lessen. When I woke up, I asked for a sign that would verify what the spiritual robe in my dream symbolized—that I would come through okay. Later, I went to an art class where the teacher picked up an artist's smock and said: 'I'm going to put a robe on you.' As she put it on me, she explained that it was the most special smock she had ever owned. The fact that she called the smock a 'robe' sent a little shock of delight through me. I knew instantly that it was the sign I was looking for."

There are a lot of ways to open yourself up to synchronistic signs. Here are just a few:

- Ask for signs out loud, with the expectation that you will receive them.

- Look for signs like a child on a treasure hunt.

- Get outside in nature with the intention of appreciating every little growing thing.

- Pay attention to numbers, coins, feathers, and other random objects.

- Pay attention to names, titles, car license plates, etc. as if you're on a magical journey.

- Notice things that others say.

- Open a book at random and point to a word with your eyes closed, then find meaning in the word.

- Journal any thoughts and impressions you have; jot down synchronistic events so you remain in the flow.

"When I was little, I saw everything as a person. The reclining chair with its heavy, padded arms and worn-out leather seat looked like someone's tired, sad old uncle to me. Everything had a human element. In the mornings before kindergarten, I'd open the sock drawer to choose which socks would accompany me to school that day. I'd instantly feel sorry for the ones that could not go with me, and especially for the lone sock who had lost its partner. I'd take out the socks I wanted and close the drawer again, reassuring the others that they'd get to come out and play soon. I'd say: 'I'm so sorry. I will wear you another day.'"

With conscious presence, you can turn any dull day into one of expectant surprise. When you cultivate an impish sense of fun by wishing for and receiving synchronistic signs, you enhance everything around you.

CHAPTER 3
SPIRITUAL
EMPATHS

The space between us is sacred. It is the approach, the port, the inhaled breath before the word is spoken. That space holds our intentions, the choices we are about to make, our hopes, our longings, our fears. It is the place where the next miracle will unfold.

Through empathy, we can fill that space with clarity and the presence of compassion. We may sense a separation between ourselves and others, but with empathy and compassion, we acknowledge our shared humanity and our common existence. We recognize that we are alive together at a specific point in time, and that we have a lot of power to bestow love, to bring goodness into our shared experiences. How we treat one another becomes, ultimately, how we treat ourselves.

This truth is perfectly expressed by Rabbi Evan Shultz in his 2021 work, "A Poem Using Book Titles in My Library" (#1):

In every generation,
In every tongue,
A time to speak.
Like dreamers—
Stepping forward,
Restoring hope,
A passion for truth.
Shared dreams,
American values,
Religious voices,
Political tribes,
Tough choices,
Broken tablets.
You're more powerful than you think
To bless the space between us.

As Rabbi Shultz so gracefully assures us, empathy makes our lives so much brighter. It makes us feel as if we are in a wondrous celebration at times. When we approach others with room to go beyond our egoic sense of pride, competition, and labeling, we fill the space between us with benevolent thoughts and compassion.

The Gift of Compassion

Spiritual empaths want to love others, even those who create conflicts. They may not like everyone or get along with everyone—and, in fact, may well steer clear of many—but they won't feel comfortable carrying negative emotions about others. This requires overriding the personality of self (and that of others) in favor of focusing on the *eternal soul essence* of the person, that which is more true than the temporary embodiment and personality they find unpalatable.

That means that empaths must attempt to live in a state that allows a current of compassion to flow for everyone, not just for those favored individuals their egos select. When empaths keep this channel open so their empathic sensing can flow easily without being blocked, they increase their intuitive knowing and they can feel this.

Empaths may suddenly receive a quiet knowing that just feels real and right to them, and then be able to share it because they have released their resistance. By contrast, the ego likes to make judgments and to be severe toward others. But empaths seek to transcend these egoic instincts and ease hardened thoughts or fears into airy potential, creating the possibility for something optimal to occur for both themselves and others. By being open and fluid, they benefit others—all others, not just those they decide are worthy.

"When the theme for a national art competition for a magazine was announced, I knew immediately that an artist I didn't really care for had recently completed a piece that would work well and that she'd be the grand prize winner. I don't know how I knew. I just saw a mental picture of the work and knew it was the winner. So I told her the piece

would be perfect for the contest. And she entered
it and she won the grand prize."

This spiritual knowingness may not always be wel-
comed by others, however. Empaths may sometimes have to
learn to share less with those who don't want to hear about
visions, impressions, or hunches. And that's fair. Although
empaths may be enthralled by wildly amazing synchronistic events that unfold, they may find that sharing
with others who are less interested in those things puts a
damper on the experience. Being empathic and intuitive
around someone who flatly denies such wonderment may
give us pause, but sometimes we just have to let others
be themselves and not hammer them with anecdotes of
empathic-intuitive scenarios. Sometimes we just have to
choose carefully to whom we communicate our spiritual
experiences and only share them with other intuitive hearts.
Empaths can always decide when and where to share.

"Is empathy the same thing as being an empath? I
often sense how others must feel, but it seems as
if sometimes others don't at all get how I feel."

So why is empathy so difficult to live by and embrace?
The idea of developing real meaningful empathy and living
a life that integrates it into the weave of our experiences and
relationships can seem radical. In fact, before even defining
what it is to be spiritually empathic, it is necessary to com-
prehend and practice empathy. But in many circumstances,
human nature disallows empathic behavior—so much so
that it seems we first learn what empathy is by knowing
what it feels like when empathy is missing.

Nobody wants to suffer alone. As we experience life's challenges, we may endure individual agonies in a way that feels sensationally isolating. Empathy is the gift we give one another to go beyond just surviving trauma. It is the essence of love and acceptance that all humans want and need. So why do we stay so focused on the pain that happens when empathy is lacking? And why do we sometimes withhold empathy from those who have offended us?

To counter these tendencies, try looking at people in a different way, through the lens of your imagination:

- *Pretend* the other person is you, and ask yourself what "your" life feels like.

- *See* others as they may have been when they were newborns, innocent and in need of love.

- *Imagine* what the other person's dream in life is—and perhaps even ask them.

Practicing viewing people and situations through your creative imagination will go a long way toward teaching you how to live the life of a true empath.

The Blame Game

Relationships are complex, and can be chaotic and emotionally confusing. People suffer most when there is a lack of humanity or compassion, and a lack of understanding in any given situation, society, or institution. Where there is little or no empathy—whether it be in the family, the school, the workplace, or the overall culture—there is angst. And that suffering cannot be overlooked.

It is usually easy to discern where and when empathy is lacking, because we know we need it to survive and to thrive. So when empathy is missing, we feel threatened to our very core. And when we feel threatened, we get defensive.

But being defensive is not a comfortable state for empaths, whose natural disposition encourages them to feel, sense, and understand the experiences of others on some unspoken level. Living life with empathy involves some extraordinary joys, as well as some excruciating (at least at first) challenges. Empaths learn to respond to a lack of empathy from others with a different sensibility than the expected and natural responses others may have in times of distress. Those who choose to honor empathic sensing and wish to develop intuitive intelligence need to be extremely sensitive and yet galvanized against negative energy and emotion. *They must be willing to avoid blaming others.*

This does not mean that they can avoid the uncomfortable task of holding others accountable or of discerning what is not acceptable by ethical standards. It does not mean that they need not protest against that which they find inhumane or somehow misguided or cruel. In fact, to be empathic is to be honest about that which does not feel right, good, healthy, or fair. Empaths generally want to call things out for what they are, even though it may disturb a lot of people and disrupt social structures when they voice their concerns.

Blaming others for causing hurt is a normal human reaction, while living empathically is often a struggle. Our approach to the idea of empathy often plays out like this: "I am hurting and want someone to know how this feels so I am not alone in my suffering." This realization is often followed by: "You are not showing me empathy. You do not know how I feel. You are not in my shoes." As human beings, we desperately want others to share our woes, while at the same time telling them that they cannot possibly know how we feel. We want it both ways—to say we suffer more than anyone could possibly register, and also to demand that others "get it."

This is the longing we carry as we yearn for a world that is more empathetic and more merciful. But this longing gets us nowhere unless we are open to living a life in which, rather than simply pining for others to feel our pain, we actively desire to practice empathy as well—and to increase this ability as time goes by. Ideally, empaths must maintain and hold dear a heartfelt willingness to feel, know, understand, and envision healing, even for those who have hurt them.

Giving and Receiving

Empaths seek to live a life of giving empathy, but they hope to receive it as well. While we typically get upset when empathy is withheld and will remember for decades those who withheld it, empaths can't be satisfied with that result, no matter how painful the ordeal may have been. It is natural to be angry or resentful when empathy is withheld, and people are often very hurt when they are denied a caring response to their predicament. Some may even want to get even. So they decide that those who failed to show empathy will get none in return. After all, they don't deserve it.

But spiritual empaths don't want the story to end there. They know that holding on to resentment can result in internal trouble. They know that if they sever themselves from the energy of compassion, understanding, and empathic sensing, they cut themselves off from forgiveness. Although it may take some time—perhaps even years—it is always worth it to them to resolve situations and to forgive others.

> "My best friend Heather told me that her fiancé said she had to choose between him and me. She chose him. I would not be her maid of honor as she had always promised, nor would I be a part of her life. It took me eighteen years to forgive her. But it took me longer to forgive myself for letting her and her fiancé hurt me like that. In the end, I realized I had to forgive her *and* myself in order to move on in my life."

This is a more difficult journey for spiritual empaths, because withholding empathy does not align with what they know to be true. No matter how badly they may want others to be punished for their ill deeds or to "get what is coming to them," empaths wish even more for an end to all suffering. In fact, they can only end their own suffering by releasing toxic emotion. Ultimately, they know that the strong negativity of anger and resentment, of withholding empathy from others, withholds it from themselves as well. And this causes them personal injury. To forgive others is to forgive yourself. Many atrocities are committed and it may be deemed that criminals do not deserve kindness or merit forgiveness. And justice is an important part of any ethical society. But empathy and forgiveness merge eventually, like two rivers, simply because survivors free themselves when they embrace empathic forgiveness, thereby releasing themselves from destructive emotions.

Empaths know intuitively that, when they feel let down by others' inability to empathize, this can be an opportunity for them to validate their own emotional and mental energy, their thoughts and feelings, their ideas and solutions. By refusing to be subject to the actions of others and rising above the ugly and cruel situations of the world, they can transcend negative energies. Karmic law assures us that what we do comes back to us. Yet there is always room for mercy to do its magic as well. Mercy and forgiveness can ease up karmic suffering for those who do the wounding; but it can also ease the pain of the wounded and end the karmic loop.

Dedication to empathic knowing does not mean unquestioned acceptance of wrongdoings or wrongdoers, however. It is rather the acceptance of the self as an entity capable of overcoming the worst in human nature. It provides the opportunity for us to live less as victims and more as the heroes of our own stories.

As life's heroic tale plays out, it can be an agonizing challenge for a sensitive soul to have to deal with other people's lack of empathy. Empaths feel this pain a thousand-fold. Witnessing atrocities and critical injuries requires action on their part because they cannot tolerate the absence of empathy, which they know will lead to a ruined world. Empaths learn that, when they carry the standard of empathic behavior, they themselves must keep to that high standard. When they wrestle with the challenge of engaging a bitter and broken world, that struggle occurs within as much as without.

Empaths can't control what people or societies do, but they can gravitate toward supporting efforts to help change systems and situations they deem unfair—perhaps one person at a time or perhaps through larger actions. And they will also welcome the blessing of a gentle snowfall of empathy from others, and be transformed by the glistening gratitude of kindness given. Empaths know that we, together, can help transcend unbearable circumstances by demonstrating genuine empathy and happily receiving it.

An old saying tells us not to hate the person, but to hate what they do. In a similar way, empaths tend instinctively to feel the humanity in others, even if their actions prove to be hurtful and destructive. In some rare and awful instances, this may seem impossible. Yet empaths will be inclined to pray for spiritual enlightenment in order to better understand the horrors of the world.

Open Hearts, Open Channels

An empath's heart always remains open. Because they know that this life is temporary and that spiritual laws are eternal, empaths are determined to live with open hearts. For them, the way through life is not to surrender to pain, but rather to meet fear, threats, and opposition with strength of heart and a shifting perspective. It takes willpower, compassion, and kindness to build this structure of inner wisdom. And it takes time and experience.

When we open our hearts, we open the intuitive channels through which empathic knowledge flows. When we look for the root cause of coarse actions that bring misery, we become enlightened. Flying over the situation to get a birds-eye view relieves our tension and allows our perspective to shift. Yet empaths know that they are always a work in progress—and so is everyone else. They know that, in the wide spectrum of frequencies of heart-centered attunement, not all people resonate with all others all the time. Everyone falls short on occasion, and playing the blame game only gives suffering more momentum. That is why living in the light and embracing positive emotions, rather than falling into the shadows and savoring negative emotions, is so pleasing. Because that is where understanding lives. That is where the chance for healing lies.

CHAPTER 4
EMPATHY AND THE EGO

Have you noticed that wise, enlightened people seem to have a sparkle in their eyes or an aura of peace about them? Everyone else may be running around in confusion, upset and anxious, but they seem calm and internally centered. They seem to have some kind of special knowledge—an observational orientation—that allows them a more relaxed and mirthful disposition. They seem to embody the essence of empathic, spiritual attunement, with its essential streak of playfulness. And this inner calm is projected outward, offering solace to others.

Seasoned empaths never appear to panic or to resist. They accept life on its own terms and exude a quality that suggests that they have already experienced the transitory nature of suffering, and are never trapped by it. They find the light in the shadows, and they bring that light from within them wherever they go, beaming it out to others.

But how can that be? Surely even the Dalai Lama curses a little when he stubs his toe! Life is excruciating and harsh for all of us at times, and some experience physical, mental, or emotional pain for long periods. Certainly, their suffering is not always by choice, but rather a condition that they must endure. Yet many confront the worst of circumstances and somehow emerge with stars in their eyes that show they have overcome painful ordeals. How do they rise out of suffering and into a feeling of well-being?

They do it by transcending the ego and releasing fiercely held ideas about themselves. And this leads them to self-renewal.

Who's the Boss?

The ego thinks it's the boss. It thinks it knows the totality of who we are. It resists suffering and cannot tolerate pain as it mediates what we think we know and what we are unconsciously learning. It refuses to accept anything it perceives as threatening. It may decide that other people are threatening, that the status quo is threatening, that differing opinions and change are threatening.

As the ego seeks to rule the empire of the self, it develops inflated ideas about itself. That is usually where our pain comes from—from the slights and afflictions felt by the ego, along with its refusal to change. Unless, of course, there is what the ego perceives as a "win" for itself! The ego detests unwelcome circumstances, so when the ego rules us, there will be trouble.

But there is also an aspect of ego that is self-abasing. It can cause us to indulge in self-sabotage as punishment, or to distort "winning" situations because it is sometimes motivated by fear, anxiety, guilt, or shame. It may cause us to be trapped in self-fulfilling prophesies and encourage us to create a comfortably painful way to experience life. Sometimes it just feels good to feel bad; sometimes we tolerate the pain we are "comfortable" with rather than risk the discomfort that comes with transformation.

This is not to say that the ego is all bad, however. Because the ego helps us to realize much about ourselves and to learn through life experience as well. In fact, our egos come in handy sometimes. We get a lot done in life pursuing the ambitions our egos generate. They help us excel; they give us the drive to make dreams come true and the courage to self-actualize as we mature. These experiences give us so much to be grateful for as we develop, even while simultaneously providing some of life's hardest lessons.

Since the ego makes some choices for us based on what we want for ourselves—what we hope for, what we desire—it is both a helper and a bringer of challenges. We are in this life to try things, so it makes sense that, within our human nature, there is an internal command center directing us along. But the ego sees only "win or lose" situations, and it always wants us to "win"—that is, to slay our opponents, to dominate every situation.

The ego seeks dominance and approval, and heartily dislikes slights and insults from others. But it also enjoys berating us from inside our own thinking when it is not praising us. Think of what happens when someone is humiliated by another's words or actions. The ego wants revenge, wants compliance, wants to attack. In its rage, it may even encourage the injured party to strike out against the offender. But the ego has no real dominion over the actions of others and the taste for revenge against others usually does not play out in ways that satisfy its ravenous desires.

The Ego's Drive to Win

Empaths struggle with egoic pain—the unresolved suffering they accumulate in life—just as others do. The difference is that they are compelled by their empathic nature to transform this pain into something beneficial, something transformative and positive. If they don't, they know intuitively that their natural attunements will go haywire, and they don't want their inner knowing to be sacrificed to the negative emotions brought on by others' actions. Moreover, egoic pride, which feeds our sense of power and self-worth, can be helpful to everyone in some ways. In the case of empaths, it can help to motivate them, because wounded pride likes to restore itself. The emerging conscious self may thus be helped by the egoic drive to win.

When we willfully initiate a process of renewal, a little bit of egoic pride may lend some vigor to the struggle to find a way out of affliction. For instance, when someone has gotten fired or lost a competition or feels degraded or is labeled unkindly by others, the ego writhes in anger and embarrassment. But soon enough, it will begin to spin a fantasy about the self becoming so indomitably successful or powerful that the person who caused the hurt will stand in amazement. And these fantasies can be powerful motivators. Inventive imaginary scenes like this may seem humorous in retrospect, but they give the ego time to recover itself a little—perhaps just enough to initiate real change.

But the motivation to welcome the possibility for renewal exists only for as long as the ego does not remain in control and able to subject the self to repeated negative episodes involving new insulters and perpetrators. The ego may cause the mind to suffer through a certain amount of spiritual evolution, a certain amount of incentive to become more conscious and empathic in life. Because empathy is the inner sensing of what *others* feel, however, and not about the self-glorification and competitive dominance of the ego, it can only survive and grow when the empathic person remains conscious of the destructive nature of the ego and constructs, over time, an inner harmony and fortitude that is not possible when the ego is in control.

When empaths start to see that they can survive letting the ego suffer a little, they achieve an inner awareness that there are greater forces at work than the ego. This allows for reflection and makes space for the breath of life—the chance to start again without needing to feel superior to others or indomitable. Much of what happens in life is not immediately understood and cannot be controlled. Empaths lean into this "not knowingness." Like sailors who adjust their sails to fill them with unseen wind or navigate by the stars at night, empaths find peace in ambiguity.

Developing empaths trust that they don't have to have all the answers or know the reasons for everything in order to make adjustments that propel them out of misery and into new clarity. This helps them to realize their own potential and to manifest the content of their dreams. The ego may cry out because it wants to maintain control, wants to win, wants to be right, wants to feel victimized. But empaths realize that this only happens at the expense of love. Why love? Because it is difficult to give love or feel love or receive love if we let the ego hold on to pain, resentment, and righteous anger.

Empathic searchers remain open to solutions, ideas, and points of view—even those that may arrive as if out of nowhere or from the strangest of sources. This openness

The Way of the Empath

disallows anger and resentment, thoughts of revenge, or fantasies of conquering the foe. Wounded empaths may have emphatic feelings, but they are inclined to work to release their reflexive grip on pain.

Sharing Empathy

It is really great fun to encourage empathic connections with others. Empathic interactions open the self and others to the possibility of a mysteriously interesting world. When the ego is not constantly checking on who is "winning" and who is "losing," there is so much space for *being* with others without fear—and this is where the fun begins. Here are just a few ways to encourage these fun interactions.

> "I asked a stranger at a bar to let me hold her ring and tell her what I saw psychically. At first, she hesitated, but then handed the ring to me. I held it in my closed palm and saw an image of a few young women leaning over a glass counter in a jewelry store, looking intently at a piece of jewelry. But the floor was dirt. That didn't seem right. But when I described this to the stranger, she told me that she and her friends had gathered in some funky jewelry place while traveling and went in to buy her a ring. They all chose it together. And the place had a dirt floor! I was just shocked. But it made me realize that I should trust my intuitive visions."

Empathic Quests
Give yourself and another person a daily "fortune-telling" by opening a book at random and pointing to the third

line down. Make that your message for the day. This kind of playful interaction is life-enhancing and fun. Share this conviviality with others by telling them you'll choose their message of the day, then take a screen shot of the page you land on.

Songs of the Heart

Another way to encourage empathic sensibility is to create "signs"—for instance, by asking for them through songs on the radio. You can do this for yourself or for a loved one. Make the next song be your message for the day, or perhaps use it to answer a specific question you or someone else may be pondering. Make sure these are lighthearted and positive exchanges.

Rock Someone's World

There is a trend many have enjoyed and been touched by, a way you can leave messages for others, kind sayings and such, by painting words on rocks. This can really give joy to others—either friends or total strangers—by providing signs where and when others need them.

> "I was having a terrible day and I found a stone on the ground. Someone had painted it with the words: 'You are loved.' I really almost started to cry. I wanted to keep it, but thought it better to leave it there and let someone else find it. Someone else might need it."

CHAPTER 5
ETHEREAL REALMS

Being transported in some way to a "reality" other than the one we find materially real in the here and now—or infusing our present reality with spiritual elements—can involve everything from astral projection and precognitive knowing, to ghosts and entities from other dimensions, to telekinesis and out-of-body experiences, to clairaudience and mediumship, to instances of déjà vu and psychometry. We may experience portals to other realms as luminescent and pearlescent spheres of light that glide through the air, or as technicolor visions of the life spiral. Some enter other realms enticed by those who have passed on, or guided by angels or other spiritual messengers. Some even visit these realms as the result of traumatic events known as near-death experiences.

All these types of experience attest to the fact that our consciousness is not a prisoner of the body it inhabits. Many report suddenly popping out of their bodies and experiencing ethereal places and spaces beyond our reality. We've all had the experience of being in an ordinary room on an ordinary day and having our minds or awareness drift to another, more abstract, kind of sensing that brings us all kinds of information and a sense of expansion beyond the corporeal. In this state, our conscious awareness opens to all kinds of mystery. Sometimes we receive this knowledge without making any effort; sometimes we intentionally seek this knowledge through practices like meditation, dream journaling, or forms of physical activity that focus our minds, like yoga. These experiences teach us that, beyond our physical presence, there exist planes of consciousness and vibrant spaces to explore. Through them, we learn that there are other worlds we can access through spiritual visions and modes of light-body (soul-body) transportation.

Spiritual Knowing

For empaths, these experiences often come in a quick flash of knowing—like images suddenly appearing in the mind's eye, or a sudden feeling of being somewhere else.

This type of empathic seeing is both fascinating and amazing. Because the spiritual-intuitive world is not subject to the rules of gravity and common causality, third-eye visions can take us on journeys in an instant, or show us images of other times, places, or events. Such experiences can be exquisitely diaphanous or oddly disturbing, depending on the type of interlude. As with all small or great miracles, they are also very personal. Things happen in the ethereal realm that cannot be explained or understood, yet they happen all the same, defying logic.

These empathic experiences can occur in many ways. Here are just a few.

Prayer

Personal prayer is an ancient, often reflexive practice that may involve chanting, intonations, and words spoken silently or aloud. Sincere prayer is a beseeching that arises from the inner depths of our being, addressed to that which we sense as a great power or omnipotent presence. Even if we do not believe in or sense the outpouring of unconditional love from a spiritual source or creator—even if we are dead to the feeling of awe—we may whisper a prayer when in the midst of great distress or fear as an expression of a most ardent desire or longing to receive divine help. It is also human to pray in gratitude for abundance received, and for miraculous turns of events.

Prayer and sacrifice seem to go together. Both honor life. When we eat, we recognize that something is sacrificed for our nourishment, be it an animal or bounty springing from the earth. The relationship between sacrifice and prayer is, in fact, a natural aspect of the human condition. We suffer in this life, yet we have the ability to overcome that suffering and to bestow upon others that gift through prayer. Gratitude, loss, hope, and mystery can all be addressed through prayer. Personal prayers that arise from the heart are emotive and can build a powerful energy that can bring healing to others, alleviate suffering, and nurture aspirations for a life lived with peace.

Regardless of our religious affiliation, or the absence thereof, prayer originates in those who implore through spiritual requests that an outcome be realized, that a sorrow or regret be overcome, or that a life be renewed in some way. Some have had ecstatic visions through prayer; some have been gifted with the expectation that their prayers will in some way be answered. And sometimes, we ourselves are the answer to someone else's prayer.

> "I knew someone who had young adult sons who required a specific and new medication to breathe. It was summer and the medication would not arrive until December, so I prayed several times a day for it to arrive sooner. I said: 'By October, please God let this medication come for them.' Summer passed and the prayer was answered! The medication arrived in October, and with a special twist. It came on the birthday of their beloved grandfather who had passed on years before. I felt my prayer was more than heard. I felt as if there were spiritual helpers surrounding us all."

Prayer is a mode of spiritual transformation because it is grounded in our own pleas, in a thread of our own souls hanging in suspension. There is something innocent about prayer and the expectation that prayers will be received and answered. This innocence makes us both vulnerable and empowered. It gives us strength through humility. It forces us to admit that, although we may not have all the answers, we are nonetheless great creators made in the image of a Great Creator. Through prayer, we can align with this powerful force as we live and evolve through life experiences. Through prayer—our spiritual knowing, our imaginal and dimensional awareness—we can draw upon our capacity to cooperate with forces outside of, yet generated from inside of, ourselves.

Out-of-Body Experiences

An out-of-body experience, or OBE, occurs when we leave our physical bodies and experience conscious awareness from a new vantage point. These events are often spontaneous and surprising, sometimes brought on by extreme pain or shock. As in astral projection (see page 60), in OBEs our consciousness is not constrained by physical and material laws. Those who experience these events often feel themselves lifted up and out, although their bodies remain breathing and alive. Some who have been traumatized by abuse as children describe leaving their bodies while the abuse was happening, leaving the painful situation and going beyond it. Others report experiencing an awareness outside of their own bodies—for instance, seeing things in other places that they otherwise would not have been able to see, and later discovering that what they witnessed was, in fact, true. Some describe a sudden physical threat that caused their souls or consciousness to exit their bodies, hover above the scene, and observe themselves below.

"I was cantering a horse when he bucked. I saw his blond mane as I soared past it and was so scared. The worst feeling of dread came over me, the dreadful feeling of knowing I was about to get hurt badly. This all happened really fast, but I seemed to experience it in slow motion. I saw the horse *from above*, which was not physically possible. I had popped out of my body. It was only maybe a three-second event, but my vision of the horse from above and the empty saddle on his back felt timeless. Then I woke up flat on my back on the ground."

Near-Death Experiences

Many people give extraordinary accounts of near-death experiences (NDEs). In these events, people who are pronounced dead, but who are revived, describe how their lives were changed by entering realms beyond their earthly reality during the time they were thought to be dead. Dr. Raymond Moody, in his book *Life After Life* (1975), explored highly spiritual episodic adventures to other realms that were described by people who had died—some even considered to be dead for several minutes or longer—only to be revived and exclaim that they had gone to another place entirely.

"I was coded during an operation. I suddenly saw myself in a beautiful place with flowers and brilliant colors that we don't have here on earth. There was a rose-covered white picket fence with a cottage behind it. At a gate in the fence, I saw my uncle who had died many years before. He was wearing a shimmering white suit and hat. He tipped his hat to me and opened the gate, saying: 'Mary, we have been waiting for you.' Before I could approach the open gate, I was suddenly back in my body."

In many NDE accounts, people describe their consciousness leaving their bodies, then observing their bodies and people all around through their spiritual bodies. These spiritual bodies—also called "light bodies" or "soul selves"—are able to go anywhere just by focusing on or thinking about it. They often report that they travel through a tunnel that leads to a pinpoint of light in the distance, as if they are being pulled along by a spiritual force. Some of these accounts include encountering guides or deities.

Almost without exception, however, those having these experiences report returning to this earthly life transformed and deeply moved. They tell of skimming the worlds between this earthly life and the next, and of visiting many dimensions. They describe meeting spiritual beings and deceased loved ones who greeted them on their journey. They tell of encounters with God, with Jesus, or with Messiah-like beings who convey unconditional love and all-knowing omnipotence.

Although these NDE events have similarities, it is also true that no two are just alike. They are each unique and very personal. Many describe being shown life reviews that play out like motion pictures in which they see everything they experienced during their lifetime. In these reviews, however, they enter the scenes and feel, not just their own feelings and thoughts, but the emotions and thoughts of all those they encounter. This leaves them highly aware of the impact they had on others, which they declare to be enormously moving and empathically impressive. Many return to life very changed and determined to live with more compassion for others.

> "I hemorrhaged during the birthing process with my fifth child. I felt myself rise up out of the bed and glide to the upper corner of the surgical theater. I felt distressed and saw all the doctors working on my body down below. Then the wall faded and I was able to see my other children in a friend's car and felt terrible. I didn't want to leave them without a mother. As soon as I thought and felt that, I was back in my body."

Astral Projection

Astral projection can occur in the dream state and in a dream-like deep meditative state. In these events, the body becomes very relaxed. A banging sound is often heard as the soul-self leaves or re-enters the body—somewhat like a big door swinging shut. This may be followed by the sound of thousands of voices, as if the soul-self were passing through a kind of purgatory on the way to somewhere else.

> "I felt I was being drawn by some force that I couldn't resist. I was moving along a road very close to the surface and could see every speck of the tarmac. It was just before dawn and I was in an unfamiliar city. All of a sudden, I was floating through someone's apartment. I was really shocked, because I knew I had no right to be there. I knew he was still upstairs sleeping and I hovered

for a little while near a dinette table on which there was a lot of electronic equipment and wires. I kept saying: 'Oh my God, I need to get out of this guy's place before he wakes up!' Eventually, the pulling motion started again and I passed through the wall and back outside. Then I woke up."

Astral projection involves lucid roaming without the physical body. Astral travelers enter a state of "light body" or soul motion that allows them to experience visions in greater detail than they normally could with their physical eyes. These journeys may take them to other cities or countries, to the homes of loved ones, or even to other dimensions, all while remaining strikingly aware that they are experiencing an astral event and enjoying heightened states of awareness and telepathic communication with other entities. Astral travelers feel a thrilling sensation, often exclaiming how unbelievable the experience is even while it is happening.

"I was in a different realm, similar to earth but more ideal. There was a pink sky and the clouds were alive—they were conscious, giggling and talking with me telepathically. There was a bay and in the bay was a dirty, dark, broken bridge. By just looking at it, I was zapped there instantly. Thoughts were all that was needed to get somewhere or to communicate. I understood the bridge symbolized earthly life, full of smoke, grime, grit, and hard lessons. Once I comprehended what the bridge represented, I zapped back to the calm shore of the bay. Everything there appeared like an animation—beautiful colors, a quality of lovely light, and a feeling of peace."

Some episodes of astral projection involve willing the self (through mental focus) to go to a specific place. In others, travelers are pulled by what feels like a mysterious magnetic force. They often feel a sense of timelessness, as if they are not bound by sequential time. Sometimes they visit what seems to be a past life or a realm of conceptual spiritual energy. Some even find that they can bring on these experiences by meditating and focusing on their desire to leave their physical bodies and explore other realms or other places on the earthly plane. Affirmations and meditations using creative visualization can help to develop this ability. By training their minds to do this, some are able to move lucidly beyond the confines of their bodies at will.

"I was talking with a Healing Touch practitioner over the phone when I started to feel as if I were in her home. I saw the interior of another house, and felt myself floating along a hallway and into a room that looked like a home office. I hovered about six feet up and saw books on a white shelf. I interrupted the reading and asked her if her house had a hallway leading to rooms including a home office with white bookshelves on the left as you entered the room. She said yes, that I had described her place exactly as it was. I had traveled to her home in the astral realm—perhaps because I had achieved a kind of trance state while listening to her talk."

Past-Life Regression

Dr. Brian Weiss, a psychiatrist at Yale University and author of *Many Lives, Many Masters* (1990), discovered that it is possible to regress patients to previous incarnations, or past lives, through hypnosis. Moreover, he discovered that events patients had endured in their past lives held the potential to heal them in their current lives. During past-life regressions, patients have described where they lived, who their family members were, and more. These scenes, re-entered while under hypnosis, often show them why they carry pain or confusion in their current lives. The first time this happened, Weiss was surprised when the patient suddenly announced that she was back in a previous life. Through guided discourse with Weiss, the patient was healed of a current health issue.

Weiss continued to explore the amazing benefits of past-life-regression therapy and found that patients can even enter future lives while in hypnotic states. Progression therapy and regression therapy are now valuable practices that offer understanding and relief to many people who need help overcoming illness or obsessive fears.

Déjà Vu

The French term "déjà vu" describes a sensation people get when they see or feel an experience as if they have seen it or felt it before. Sometimes people describe sensing in the moment that they have been somewhere or experienced something in the past. They report that a rush of familiar sensation overcomes them that they cannot explain. It is as if what they are doing in the moment was known to them before in the exact way they are currently experiencing it. Some consider this to be a spiritual sign of being on track with life, as though it is a momentary nod to the soul that plans being made will be fulfilled—a kind of mystical pat on the back as if to say: "You are living life exactly as your soul chose to prior to your current incarnation." These events are hard to describe and are often gone as quickly as they came. Nevertheless, they can be compelling and powerful to those who experience them.

Precognition

Many people have precognitive experiences in which, for some unexplained reason, they get a glimpse of events that then unfold in real time just as shown in the vision. There is no rational or logical explanation for these occurrences, and they are often baffling and surprising to those who experience them, and to others who may witness them. After all, although the process cannot be explained, the result often cannot be denied. It is almost as if events in time have an unexpected elasticity.

Those having precognitive visions may recognize them as "other"—as something notably different when compared to memories or to other more ordinary mental pictures created in the mind. They may come as dreams or quick flashes of mental imagery. While it may be possible to enter into a meditative state and receive precognition, it is only with hindsight that precognitive visions can be validated. Nobody has the final say over their own or other people's possible future events. (Sometimes a suggestion may preceed the outcome, so caution is advised.)

"When I was in graduate school, I dreamed I walked up to the classroom door and found a note that said class was cancelled because the teacher had a toothache. Then, in the dream, I saw someone throwing up and I even smelled the vomit. The next morning, I was walking down the hallway at school with a classmate when we both saw a note on the door about twenty feet away from us. When my classmate wondered what it was, I said it was a note saying there would be no class because the teacher had a toothache. She walked up to the door and read the note, then turned to me and asked: 'How did you know that?' I answered: 'Oh, I just know these things.' As I walked back to my car, I ran into another classmate and told her there was no class that day. She answered: 'I am so glad, because I was up all night throwing up!'"

Mediumship

Mediums are those who see, hear, or feel the presence of others who are no longer alive on earth. These experiences may come visually, by hearing the voice of a loved one, or through signs, synchronicities, and dreams. Some even tell of seeing objects that appear to have moved.

"We were finally moving my father out of his house to live with my oldest sibling. It had been almost six years since my mother had passed away and his memory was failing and his health slipping. He seemed lost without her. When we were making his bed that night in his new bedroom, we opened a box we had moved from a remote corner closet in their home and I was astounded to find a set of pillows with freshly laundered cases on them, as if they had been waiting for us to place them there for him! It was a gift and a message from my mother, and we knew he was where he was supposed to be."

Others have shared mediumship experiences in which a deceased loved one appears simultaneously to them and to another close relative or friend. Some have even experienced these events using technological devices.

"I was in deep grief and texting someone telling them how hard my life was, and how much I was hurting and struggling. I had to give my son his dinner, so I tapped out: 'I will be right back.' Later, I picked up the phone and, in the space where I would have typed a new message, I found the words: 'I am so sorry.' I was shocked because I knew I hadn't typed that! I knew then that my loved one had sent me a message to comfort me."

Ghosts and Other Discarnate Spirits

Ghosts may be the wandering spirits of those who once lived, but have been gone for a while. There is no sense of sequential time in the spirit realms like what we experience in our earthly lives, so it is possible that these spirits exist only in an eternal "now," in which they may feel somewhat lost. Some seem curious; others continue toiling as they did while alive as if they have not left their bodies. Some appear injured in some way, signaling to those who perceive them that they are suffering from unresolved pain. Some of these spirits literally glisten with life, hovering a few feet above floor level. Some appear as holograms or like colorful animations.

"I saw a teenage girl from the 1970s hovering beside the bed. She had a tart attitude and appeared almost real. Her skin glowed. Her hairstyle had 'wings.' What stunned me is that, when I saw her, she felt my stare and then lifted her eyes to mine. She turned to look at me before disappearing. Either her energy sensed mine or she heard my thoughts."

There are ghosts of all kinds. Some carry negative energy and hope to feed off the energy of the living by frightening them. Some are simply full of mischief. And some may even be protective, warning us of hazards or future pain.

"Not long after my mother died, I woke up one morning and distinctly heard her call out my name. It was her voice, loud and clear. I wasn't sure why I heard her, however. Then later, when I was at the airport, a snow storm hit and my flights kept getting canceled. Then there was a rush on hotels because everyone's flights were canceled. Several hours later, I was still trying to find a hotel for the night. It was then that I understood. I felt as if my mother had seen what was coming for me and had called out my name so I'd know that she was in some way with me. I felt comforted by this, by her."

It is also possible that our consciousness survives us after death in whatever state it was in while we lived. If this is true, the energy of discarnate spirits will potentially mirror the energy that was present at the moment of death. Popular media loves to exploit our fears about ghosts who carry negative energies and suffering into the afterlife. But we all control what we allow in our immediate presence. If you do not want to see scary ghosts, don't allow them in. Affirm your space as your space. Energetically, your space is yours and you can determine what you admit.

Clairaudience

Clairaudience occurs when a sound or a voice is heard telepathically or with extra-sensory perception. In these events, we hear things inter-dimensionally as if we were hearing them directly—even though direct auditory input is impossible in the circumstances. Often, these sounds seem to be heard or discerned *inside* the ear drum, as opposed to being heard in the area surrounding the ears.

> "I went to a cute café that had formerly been a firehouse. As I sat at the table, I heard the chair beside me scoot back. I assumed someone had kicked it backward, moving it a few inches. Then I realized there was nobody else there. I looked around, not believing it. When the waitress came by, I asked her if she ever experienced strange things there or heard unusual sounds in the place. She nodded and said that every morning when she arrived before anyone else, she heard noises that she could not explain."

Angels and Spirit Guides

Guardian angels and spirit helpers guide and protect us. Sometimes we are even able to perceive them. Many experience voices guiding them to safety or advising them in dangerous situations. Some feel as if something or someone is gently nudging them to go one way rather than another, only to later find out that the direction not taken was hazardous in some way.

> "I was using a defibrillator on a man who was having a heart attack. The defibrillator backed up on me and the electric shock was so powerful that I could not let go of the handles. I was surrounded by a bright light, as if I had entered another space. Then I distinctly heard a male voice command me: 'Let go of it!' But I still could not let go. Then I heard the voice again: 'Throw it!' I somehow released the handles and they went flying across the room. I know it was my guardian angel who saved my life that day."

Creative Imagining

A life devoid of empathic sensing is a life that denies the power of the imagination to innovate. Yet even those most resistant to empathic sensing describe experiencing events that seemed to defy logic. We all recall with an inner glow times when we've been playfully imaginative or sensed an otherworldly presence or surprising insight. Empaths seek out these creative and imaginative experiences as a pathway to the etheric. While we all may experience sudden

involuntary moments of déjà vu, empaths cultivate a predisposition to otherworldly experiences that propel them into an open-hearted, intuitive realm. Their imaginations allow them to enter this realm by creating and co-creating it.

Some people consider the imagination an "extra" component to life—almost like an after-thought, an add-on to the more important things in life. They think of imaginative thought as "child's play." But the imagination should be valued far more highly than that, because it is where our own creative vision and powers exist. The imagination functions, not beside material life, but interwoven with it. Imaginal vision is essential for wholeness and gives birth to invention, solutions, and great works of expression.

Most things created in our material world existed in this imaginative-creative realm long before they were given physical form. And this is true of everything—the chairs we sit on, the dwellings we live in, the art and music we enjoy, the literary creations and scientific discoveries that enthrall us and enhance our lives. These are all the offspring of the human imagination. Creating with third-eye vision is a powerful means by which we can build a more ideal life. And this includes encouraging a deeper connection of human-to-human compassion and building a responsible relationship with nature. Imagination opens the heart and mind to compassion. It provides a magnified awareness. It supplies a wider recognition of varied human experiences.

For intuitive people, empathic impressions and strong sensations abound in and are an integral part of the mundane world. Through them, empaths can enter into a sudden heightened awareness, as if zapped through a spiritual portal into an etheric realm.

Keeping the heart open to spiritual experiences is an exercise in empathic expansion. We call on these experiences often in our dream state, but we can also intentionally ignite them—just as, when we walk into a store and smell the strong aroma of cinnamon, it calls up memories of autumn and winter holidays.

CHAPTER 6
SPONTANEOUS KNOWING

We often experience the ethereal through a kind of spontaneous knowing that places us exactly where we need to be at the precise moment we need to be there in order to benefit from advantageous occurrences that we could not have orchestrated ourselves. These events often lead to deeper empathic knowledge, because they make us realize that there is more going on than what appears on the surface. This empathic, mystical knowing arrives in an instant, sometimes with results that we and others consider miraculous. Artists refer to these spontaneous events as "happy accidents."

Happy Accidents

Happy accidents occur when, somewhere along a creative, empathic process, a surprise is unveiled. Through a series of small steps—perhaps precognitive (or predestined?) or seemingly arranged by some other force—we are led to an unexpected outcome and wonderment unfolds. These events may only be noted for their significance after the fact. Those who experience them may be "accidental empaths," having undergone a wildly surprising spiritual experience that confounds and amazes them. They may even feel that they have witnessed an unexplained bit of magic. Many have described the events leading up to this spontaneous knowing as life-saving or life-changing.

> "I told my daughter I'd bake cookies for her. But I woke up that morning thinking I'd skip making the cookies so I could rest in bed longer. Then something in me urged me to just go ahead and get up and bake the cookies. As I entered the kitchen, I heard the loudest crashing sound. A tree had fallen through the house in my bedroom! If I had still been in bed, I would have been struck dead by that tree."

Our empathic knowing strongly connects us to the fecundity of nature. Often, the quiet knowing nestled in that oneness shows us how connected we are to the elements and the wider world. We sense a shared harmony with the world around us and feel protected from the dangers and violence with which the natural world is fraught. Sometimes these empathic messages prepare us for taking action. They work with our animal instincts as we occasionally struggle with our human nature, or deal with choices made by others that impact us. Empathic clues give us precognitive hints that help us protect ourselves, whether by a sense of foreboding or a series of perplexing conditions we do not understand until after the episode has unfolded.

> "It was a warm September evening and I had the windows open in the house. I could not sleep. I tossed and turned; I meditated; I tried everything. Finally, I got up and shut and locked all of the windows. About a half hour later, I heard an intruder on my back deck. I know what my body feels like when it senses danger and goes into protective mode. It has happened twice since. I feel it and I go into fight mode."

Sleep disturbance and acting within the flow of it in this case saved someone from a possibly terrible outcome. But finely tuned empathic awareness can set off a series of small steps that, taken together, lead to some very good outcomes as well. Being flexible enough to flow with moments as they come and go allows us to notice spontaneous good surprises as they enter our lives. Consider the case of the woman who took the wrong way to the coffee shop.

"I wanted coffee one morning and, although I knew how to get to the place, for some weird reason, I took first one wrong turn and then another. When I stopped at an intersection to let a pedestrian walk safely across, he motioned for me to go ahead and I shouted out the window: 'No, people first, not cars!' He laughed and, the next thing I knew, we were talking and exchanged cards. I was so glad I had met him and I never would have known he existed if I had taken the right route. I knew in my heart that I was supposed to connect with that person."

Staying in the Flow

Empaths suffer when they become locked into rigid time-lines and demanding schedules. They need a more ser-endipitous disposition to feel plugged into the universal empathic zone. There are times when a strict schedule is necessary, of course. But in general, most empaths prefer an organically supple schedule and don't take well to an overly regulated existence. Empaths can work within structures, but their sensitivity requires that they avoid rigidity. They need to welcome spontaneous interactions with others, and to focus on people rather than schedules or systems.

Empaths work best when their movements are volun-tary, not etched in stone. Because they go with the impres-sions they're receiving, strict schedules may interfere with the strong feelings they may get to break the routine. This is not the same as succumbing to a willful impulse or engag-ing in something potentially destructive or damaging. It is rather that empaths feel a physical resistance mounting inside when something they are planning to do does not feel right.

> "I dreaded the event that was planned. No part of me wanted to do it. I felt this in my limbs, in my trunk—my entire body was telling me 'no.' I was so glad when the other person called and said they had to cancel. I don't know if I was picking up on their inability to meet, or if my intuition was telling me it wasn't the right timing. I do know how relieved I was when I got to avoid it."

Just as nature can be orderly—mowed, clipped, and groomed—empaths can be disciplined and grounded, yet welcome a hint of chaos in their lives. In fact, a life that feels hedged and trimmed, but with room for some uncultivated space that has a wild beauty and a feeling of spontaneous expression may be the best empathic environment for sensitives.

Within the unpredictable, moments of pre-cognition and quiet knowing can occur. An overly precise or regimented life leaves no room for random thoughts, ideas, or happenings. It tends to ignore intuitive thoughts, creative urges, and spontaneous feelings that arise. Many occupations leave little room for randomness, while others adapt well to it. Anything to do with children, for instance, allows for creative thought and action because children are naturally spontaneous and curious. They are expressive and often without guile, at least until they are trained not to be so. Spending time with children is good for empaths. Even the most exhausted empathic parent will delight in the playful surprises that come with young children.

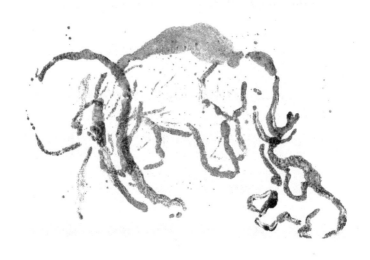

The Five Senses

In an environment that allows spontaneity and surprises, empaths can indulge their "sixth sense"—their way of knowing that goes beyond the five senses. Through this kind of intuitive knowing, they can embrace so much more than what the five physical senses can deliver. Yet the five senses can act as portals to ethereal realms as well, to dimensions of quiet knowing. Each of the senses can serve as a vehicle for transporting us through time. With one slight scent or sound or taste or texture or image, we may suddenly find ourselves where we were decades ago—and with substantial emotional impact. When this happens, we are in an ethereal moment, as if no time has passed between the initial exposure to the sensory stimuli and the present moment.

Because our physical senses direct so much of our earthly experience, we are subject to these unexpected moments of transcendence. We cannot anticipate these altered states, because they often come very unexpectedly. But we can play along with them and celebrate their abstract nature. Curiosity guides us to them, just as déjà vu strikes us unprepared. Indeed, opportunities to experience these moments of intuitive and quiet knowing abound.

An empathic orientation to life requires that we remain open to the unexplainable and the mysteriously ethereal. Just as when we enter a dream state, empathic attunement can open a portal to other places, spaces, and times. Empaths revel in the unexpected shifts that come with this passage, simply because it feels so adventuresome.

The five physical senses can snap us into these unexpected moments of empathic focus. They can act as time machines because of the powerful impressions they make on us. One whiff of a peppermint breath freshener may take a person back in time to a winter blizzard experienced during childhood, decades ago. While standing on a hot sunny bluff in the summer, the scent may trigger a stark memory of someone putting a candy cane into a hot cup of cocoa.

All the senses can activate memories and emotions as if no time has passed. Through them, we are easily transported to other places and times, complete with all the feelings and emotions we had at the time of the initial event. Here are some simple experiments you can do to experience the power of the physical senses. Start with the sense of smell, then move on to the other four. Connect empathically with all five senses, and make a note of the influence that each has on you as you recall the past.

Smell

Try using different scents to see if they trigger different memories. Have you walked into a place that has a certain scent and instantly been reminded of a childhood experience or a loved one? Did you recall time spent with a grandmother, for example, almost as if you were there?

> "When I was very young, I felt nervous and afraid when my mother went out to a party or to dinner with my dad (a rare treat for them) and left my older siblings in charge. It made me feel insecure because everything seemed wild and out of control compared to the calm atmosphere my mother maintained around the house. Mom always used a particular perfume when she went out to dinner. When I detected it in the air, I'd run into her room and watch her get ready, dreading her departure. To this day, if I smell that perfume, I feel that same hint of anxiety again."

Gather random items—grass cuttings, essential oils, articles of clothing, something made of leather, an item of food—and place them all in front of you on a table. Then follow these five steps as you consider each individual scent:

- *Journal it.* With a journal open and ready to record the impact of each sensory item, pick them up one by one and smell each one with your eyes closed.

- *Experience it.* Breathe in the scent. You may get an immediate impression, memory, or feeling that you recognize powerfully, or you may experience more subtle notions.

- *Welcome the nonsensical.* You may get random and seemingly inconsequential or irrational and unrelated thoughts, feelings, and associations. These impressions are frequently present in the dream state, which is not so different from the daydream state you are in now. Allow for and receive all the impressions that arise into your awareness, even if they do not seem to make sense.

- *Honor your feelings.* Consider all your feelings, mental images, and thoughts to be completely valid. Those that may seem illogical often hold the most empathic treasure, because they connect your inner world to the outer world through channels of which you had not been conscious before.

Once you have experienced each scent to its fullest and considered the impressions you receive, ask yourself these questions:

- *Does this item smell good to me?* If so, think and feel about why it smells pleasing. If it smells unpleasant to you, do the same. Be present for a while and consider why you reacted the way you did. Linger with the impressions you get. What do they remind you of?

- *Do I get any surfacing memories from the scent?* If you do, jot them down. If not, consider the kind of association you do have with the smell. Make sure that you focus on the smell of the item first, and not the facts about it. For example, write about how the smell affects you, not about the functional relationship you may have with the item. You can focus on the reason for the item being in your life, because that is a big part of your overall impression, but first emphasize the feelings you have.

- *Does the smell remind me of a person, location, or time?* If it does, savor it for a moment for the sake of the intuitive and empathic resources it may give you. Write down anything that comes into your thinking. Even if it seems unconnected or irrational or illogical, write it down anyway while you allow the feelings to exist within your conscious attention.

- *How does the smell of the item make you feel?* Then consider its use for you or its reason for being in your life. What associations or feelings and thoughts do you have about it?

Once you have written down your impressions, take a moment to explore how the ideas that surfaced, including the ones that seemed disconnected or irrational, actually are connected. One way to do this is to explore inwardly all the ways in which the nonsensical response makes you feel. Then connect that impression with other times you may have had that same feeling. Linking the impression up to all your other feelings about the smell can give you an interesting picture.

Here is an example:

"I picked up an old book and closed my eyes. Then I opened it and took in a big whiff. I instantly thought of school days and felt uncomfortable, which surprised me. I guess because I was nervous a lot in school. Maybe test anxiety and all that. Then I saw in my mind the color beige, which I realized was because there was a lot of beige in public schools—the walls, the paint on the legs of chairs, even the tile floors.

"I breathed in again and noticed that the smell reminded me of how often I had felt hungry in school. When I wrote all this down, I realized I was almost always starving in school, probably from eating a rushed breakfast and then waiting for hours until lunch. The smells of the cafeteria food wafted down the hallways, and sometimes it was a few hours before it was lunchtime. I'd be so hungry waiting for lunch that I was distracted.

"So now I think the color beige and the smell of cafeteria food warming up and old book smells are all in one place in my mind, with a vaguely disappointing feeling because I was uneasy in school and that led to feeling down on myself."

When you round out your feelings and couple them with your thoughts, you create space for empathic knowing to arise through reflection on those subtle emotions and thoughts. Through feeling and being present in that powerful memory moment, you create connections with mental imagery like colors. This allows your central nervous system reactions and the shaping of your persona as influenced by these stimuli to merge. In the process, you achieve a deeper self-understanding and open up a world of wisdom simply by paying attention in an empathic meditation.

Now, using these same basic steps, journal about all the other senses and see if that empathic reflection opens you to connections you did not consciously know were made. Then link these connections with perceptions about yourself and others, or about the environments that have influenced you over the years.

Taste

We all know what we like and what we don't like. It is rare that we force ourselves to eat foods we detest. In fact, you probably already know what flavors you prefer. So for this experiment, try foods that are familiar as well as some you have never tried before. Gather a range of foods to taste one by one and reflect in your journal about the powerful reactions you get in the way of immediate responses, memories, associations, and emotions that surface. You can also bring your journal to each meal and savor the flavors of the food while writing down 'the precise responses you have to them. Try to go beyond just stating whether or not you like them.

> "It was a big family dinner and there were these red beets that looked like blood on my plate. I felt sick just looking at them. My parents said that I did not have to eat them if I did not like them, but that I had to try them at least. Finally, I tasted them and got sick right then and there. The earthy smell and flavor was too much, but it was the look of them that put me off the most. But now I eat beets with no trouble."

Touch

The sense of touch is very sensual for us because we have so many nerve endings on the surface of our skin that make us sensitive to changes in texture and temperature. This protects us from dangers like high heat or extreme cold, as well as from engaging with sharp objects. Some people even avoid touching surfaces that look like a texture that repels them. Some cringe if asked to touch something that suggests unpleasantness to them—gooey globs of glue or slimy objects like worms or wet fish.

"I can't stand the feeling of chalk on my skin!"

One way to experiment with the sense of touch is to use a "touch box." Cut a hole big enough to put your fist through in one side of a cardboard box. Have someone else place some items with various textures inside the box. Alternatively, you can dedicate a separate box to specific kinds of texture—soft things, rough things, smooth things, etc.

Because you are not able to see what you are touching and you don't know exactly what the objects are, your sense of touch will be heightened in anticipation of the unknown. As you feel the objects in the box, enjoy describing how they feel and how they make you feel. What images or impressions do they call up in your imagination or in your memories? What thoughts spring up when you touch them?

"I noticed my son, when he was a toddler, reacted to the texture of sand. I thought he'd like it and play with it, but he withdrew his hands quickly, not liking how it felt at all."

You can also try setting up a touch box for someone else so you can observe their reactions and participate in their reflections. You can adapt this experiment by using smaller boxes with ventilation holes to test the sense of smell. Place spices or cotton balls soaked in strong aromas inside.

Hearing

We all hear words or music that make strong impressions on us. Sound, in fact, fills our days. A song on the radio, for example, can place us instantly in the time when we initially experienced that same song, and this impression can be powerful enough to transport us there. A song can take us back to childhood, not just as an anecdotal memory, but with the same emotions that we felt at that time in life.

> "I grew up in an industrial town and heard trains in the night, switching tracks, coming and going. I also heard nearby birds singing. But I forgot all about that after I moved away. Later in life, when I was recovering from an illness and was told to get a lot of fresh air, I sat outside and heard birds singing. Then I heard a train in the distance. And it brought me back to my childhood in an instant. I felt like that kid again for a few moments."

Clairaudience is another way of hearing sounds, similar to seeing third-eye images that are received with the eyes closed. Empaths are often clairaudient. They are very sensitive to sound and many describe hearing messages inside their heads. They may think they hear footsteps or someone calling their names, only to find nobody there. In these cases, sound can act as an entry or portal into the ethereal realm of disincarnate beings or as spiritual communication.

> "We were in the room down the hall watching television. I heard the carport door close, then footsteps, then kitchen cupboards opening and closing. I told my sister that our brother must be

home. During the commercial break, I walked into the kitchen expecting to see my brother, but nobody was there. I reported this to my brother-in-law the next day and he told me that the woman who had previously owned the house had gone to the grocery store one day. As she headed home, her car hit a gas main and she died. From then on, we were sure it was her ghost making those noises in the kitchen."

There are many ways in which sound can transport you. In fact, silence itself can be a trigger. White noise in particular can transport you somewhere else entirely. It is almost as if what you hear lies beneath the sound of the white noise itself. Some say they hear singing or talking in white noise. Some report that white noise makes them feel as if they are zooming through outer space. Try listening to white noise with your eyes closed. You can turn on a vacuum cleaner or hair dryer, or sit by an air conditioner. Let the generic sound bring you to a meditative state. Be as relaxed as you can be and see if you hear something "other."

Music of all kinds moves us greatly. Try using music to experiment with sound, then journal about it and reflect on its power to shoot you off into another zone.

Sight

Our eyes transport us constantly to other places. When we see a photograph of a faraway island, we can project ourselves there instantly. Even if we are just looking at a page in a magazine, we can find ourselves digging our toes into the hot sand, feeling the balmy salty sea breeze under an azure sky, hearing the waves crash, and smelling flowers (or coconut oil, or sunscreen). We may even get a jolt of the taste of our favorite cocktail. All this from just glancing quickly at an image on a page.

Our sense of sight is highly developed because it supports our survival; we find the best food, see into the distance to detect possible danger, and make choices that are seriously influenced by what we see. Because of this, we can easily be manipulated by visual imagery. Our society uses this brilliantly to get us to buy products. It lures us with sultry images or fear-based ads telling us we don't look right, or that we need this or that in order to be happy. Billions of dollars are made annually using visual imagery to entice and snag us.

But vision can also have a tremendous healing effect on us. The vibrational frequency of colors can be soothing, exciting, healing, and motivating. In fact, color has a far more powerful influence on us than we realize. Empaths especially benefit from color and the power it has to evoke feelings.

Here are some ways in which you can experiment with the effects that color and visual images can have on your life:

- *Color wall.* Paint one wall in your favorite color and see if it lifts your mood.

- *Color cards.* Cut magazines or cloth into squares and glue them onto index cards. Then just play with the cards. Pair them; let the vibrational resonance of each color enter your consciousness.

- *Word pairs.* You can even be playful with the visual images that words call up. Write down twenty adjectives, twenty nouns, and twenty verbs on separate index cards. Place them in separate piles, according to parts of speech. Choose one from each pile to create a funny grouping of words that stimulates a visual image. For example: Plaid Cat Singing.

Synesthesia

Synesthesia occurs when two or more of the senses blend in a single perception. The mixing of one sense with another leads to rich overlapping sensations, thoughts, and feelings. When sounds, tastes, scents, textures, and sights are woven into a single thought or impression, it can result in a complex tapestry of imaginative sensing. This happens instantaneously for some, and this can be rare gift. Empaths often experience synesthesia—for example, sometimes seeing colors that go with numbers or letters of the alphabet, or sensing smells with sounds, or textures with flavors, or colors with words. In fact, there is no limit to the potential couplings and groupings that can spring from sensory-inspired merging when it occurs naturally and spontaneously.

It is also possible to develop some synesthetic ability through playful meditative reflection on the five senses and by consciously registering any associations one sense may have that opens to another. The trail of discovery often leads to possible logical explanations for synesthetic events—for example, when a food color also has a strong taste and smell. It is easy to see, for example, how apples and cinnamon might be synthesized in the mind because they are often paired in cooking And since apples are red, the color red may bring to mind the smell of cinnamon. The same might be true for lemons and the color yellow.

But there are far more seemingly unrelated sensory matches that can only be understood by the individual making the associations. For empaths, who are naturally prone to synesthesia, the world is a feast of all the senses blending together, often conjuring up very unique and creative ideas, regardless of how unlikely or incompatible they may seem. Here are some examples:

- "My aunt reminds me of a lamp. Don't ask me why, she just does. A standing lamp with a tilting lamp shade." (A memory of a person blends with the personality of a visual object.)

- "Just looking at the color pea green makes my skin crawl." (Color blends with texture.)

- "The sound of a single flute makes me think of the color kelly green." (Sound blends with color. Perhaps the flute evokes birds singing on a summer day, which calls up an image of lush greenery.)

- "My friend and I ordered a pudding dessert that made me think of fevers and headaches and the *I Love Lucy Show* because it tasted exactly like baby asprin! When I was home sick from school, I'd lay in bed with old reruns on television with the taste of baby asprin lingering on my tongue. It is unlike any other flavor, until this pudding!" (A range of memories connected through a flavor recalled from childhood opens the senses to visual memories and tactile or physical sensations of being unwell.)

- "Heavy-metal rock music makes me see in my mind all kinds of clashing violent scenes and makes me feel awful, as if my body is under threat. I imagine this is what hell sounds like." (Sound triggers potent visual imagery and a visceral response.)

- "The color pastel blue reminds me of the number 7 and a feeling of lightness for some reason." (The simple linear appearance of the number 7 registers as uncomplicated, light, and airy, blending with the notion of the open sky.)

- "This one soda pop flavor is awful to me because it tastes like the smell of a gas station bathroom." (Taste reflexively recalls an unpleasant and seemingly unrelated smell.)

CHAPTER 7
CHANGING
PERCEPTION

Viktor Frankl, Holocaust survivor and author of *Man's Search for Meaning* (2006), gave us a gift of great wisdom when he wrote of enduring inhumanly extreme conditions: "When we are no longer able to change a situation," he notes, "we are challenged to change ourselves."

But changing ourselves, our perception, is not a comfortable process. We are often resistant to change, whether it be to situations that are out of our control (which lead to forced change) or to change that is desperately needed but delayed. Our perceptions of ourselves do evolve as we evolve, but, as we work within a developed structure of self-perceptions, we tend to function within that existing structure. This makes truly difficult alterations to the structure uncomfortable.

Sometimes life seems to knock down our inner concept of self and who we thought we were. When this happens, the world we thought we knew is destroyed. When our perception of the world is no longer what it was, we witness who we thought we were from a different perspective, and this can make our idea of our former selves seem illusory.

Perceptions of Self

Our perceptions of self are formed early in life. From the time we are newborn infants and throughout our stages of maturation, we absorb everything we see, hear, touch, taste, and smell. These impressions help build us into a world of our own based on information that comes together from the outside and is regulated within us. Our choices, preferences, and lives in general are thus greatly impacted by our perceptions. We gather information and formulate concepts that are associated with a blend of influences that all come together to structure our sense of who we are in the world and what the world is for us.

This is, in part, how we learn to discern and to have opinions, preferences, and leanings. We even build our identities from the amalgamation of the ideas we form, even though they may be prejudicial. For example: "I was born in a small town; this makes me a country bumpkin." Sometimes we surprise ourselves and outgrow the ideas that others have of who we are, as well as our own notions about ourselves. But sometimes we remain veiled to the fact that we might enjoy life more if we transitioned from old self-concepts and tried a new way of seeing who we have become. The perception we have of ourselves can, in fact, be a trap if it is constrained by any constructs or preconceived ideas.

Empaths are usually extremely sensitive to the impressions they gather and often find it hard to override them, to move into a new way of seeing things. Some memories may be too strong to shake off. Trauma has a way of defining us; we allow it to do this because our suffering makes a mighty impression on us. Empaths—and really all of us—can come to be owned by their pain, because personal experience carves into us so deeply that it is hard to separate the essence of our spiritual being from the implications of the events that shape us. But we are not defined by these events; we are ever-forming and ever-evolving beings. We are a coming together of many forms of energy and not fixed objects. And even fixed objects are made of energy. We liken ourselves at times to a stagnant pond when we are, in fact, more like an ever-flowing river moving along powerfully over and around obstacles.

Most people know what it is like to experience something traumatic and find it hard to forget the details of the experience. Some are so profoundly affected by events that they carry unimaginable pain inside themselves for years—sometimes even for their whole lives. Some may seek to relieve their suffering through substances like alcohol or drugs. When the burden of the torment becomes too heavy, the impulse to get relief, even if only temporarily, is strong. But after the high comes the let-down. The suffering returns, no evolutionary shift in perception occurs, and true relief is never realized. Self-perception in relation to the trauma is not altered.

And just as we are not the bad things that happen to us, neither are we the advantages we may have been given. We are not our money, our status, or our collections of material things, although we can so easily imagine ourselves to be. We may see ourselves reflected in the things that surround us, but we are not defined by them. Even if they become symbols of self-identity, they are not reliable signifiers, since they can all be taken away, leaving only who we are energetically at our core—a being who is continually becoming.

Agents of Change

Empaths do well when they dedicate some time each day to centering and realizing that self-perception and the way we see the world is very elastic, if only we can release our grip on it. Some ways in which we look at ourselves or others or the world around us cease to serve us as we grow. So it can be very helpful to activate a natural method of centering and grounding throughout the day. Here are some simple practices that can help keep you in touch with your empathic self.

Breath of Life

Focusing on the breath is a simple way to release thoughts that continually feed your notions of self. The psyche needs a break from thinking, from self-labeling, from worrying and remembering. A discipline of conscious breathing can help here, because it harmonizes your mind-body-spirit connection. Some forms of spiritual or physical action combined with meditation (like yoga or Tai Chi) work well, because they focus on breath and on moving the body with focused attention. This gives your mind some free space and your heavy heart some air.

Practices that involve a focus on breathing with intention (deeply, slowly) relax the nervous system and make room for possibility and potential. Sometimes all you have to do is to breathe deeply for five to ten minutes and let your perception of self disengage itself from the dictates of your mind. Breathing lets your heart ease and your inner world quieten a little. You don't have to solve every problem or come up with the answers to every question. When you meditate with deep breathing, things just start falling into place, as if the breath itself makes way for change. New perception begins to show itself, like a flower unfolding. This is not to say, of course, that a few breathing exercises will fix serious trauma, PTSD, or other similar conditions. But focused breathing has a way of positioning you to empower yourself and realize life in a way that feels better for you.

Empaths especially need to practice forms of meditation because of the heavy load of energies they absorb. So take a walk, ride a bike, dance around, do yoga, knit—anything that helps you to breathe into a better feeling place.

Color Theory

Some impressions are oppressive; they can leave you under a shadow. But life is ever-changing. So if what you see all day seems never-changing, it may help to jazz things up a little. We all benefit when we welcome adjustments, exhibit flexibility, and adapt to change. Altering the visual, physical

appearance of things is one way to step into renewal, since what we see with our physical eyes impacts our idea of "the way things are" in our minds.

Try choosing new colors for your dwelling. Even a new pillow in a color or pattern you like but don't currently have around can help. And what about changing up your wardrobe or even your hair? Alter your "I am" notions to "I am all new" notions by shifting the colors in your life. You will notice how excited people can be when doing something new with their environment or appearance. You are not your rooms or your house or your physical features, but that stuff can keep you stuck in the idea of who you *think* you are. And it can be fun to play with those perceptions.

Shove It!

We are creatures of habit. So it's easy to get stuck in the rut of our own perceptions and overlook or never see ways around and through some aspects of life. You can get heavy without realizing it, and begin to feel as immobile as furniture that can't move itself. One way to create a shift in perspective is to scan your immediate environment and change up the energy in it by moving the furniture around.

If you have no way of really re-working how the energy flows in a room because of space limitations, try a simple adjustment. Even taking one chair and shoving it a little more at an angle or moving it up or back a foot can reassert your will to declare an energy conversion. Make small moves and gestures—open a few doors or windows to let a cool breeze blow through. Clean up the place, perhaps with a new essential oil you have not used before to introduce a new scent into the air. Move small objects around. Concentrate on some intentions while you do this, and feel the air of change come upon you.

Upside Down

Seeing things upside down is strangely good for us. Gravity and its effects on the placement of self and objects tends to let our enviroments become set in stone. But looking at things upside down can give you a break from the norm. Try lying on your back on a bed (bean bag chairs work too) and letting your head tilt close to the edge, but not so close that you strain your neck. Keep your eyes open. Now explore the room upside down. Look around; take your time; gaze softly.

Or use a yoga mat and do some stretches that position your head upside down, then look around. What feelings does this give you? People often come up with new ideas and blends of unexpected thoughts simply because they flip their world on its head.

Let your upside-down time be a meditation on perceptual orientation. This may seem useless at first, but if you hang out with it a little, with seeing things differently (literally), you send a signal to your mind that there are other ways of perceiving the world than the ways you are used to. Children instinctively put themselves in upside-down positions frequently at play, simply because they are so well attuned to a creative-perceptive response to their environment.

Elevation Change

We primarily notice things that are at about eye level without really realizing it. But you can learn a lot by trying to see your world from above, from a "bird's-eye view." Try standing (safely) on a chair or ladder or balcony, and looking down. You may see all kinds of things from up there that you didn't know were there. Now go in the opposite direction and get down on the floor. What does the room look like from way down below? It is another universe! Anytime you alter your visual plane, you open your senses and perceptions. This is good for the mind because it sends a message of excitement and freedom. You do not have to be subject to your cemented-in notions of the places and spaces you traverse and inhabit.

Light Show

We respond powerfully to light and color; they churn our emotions. Moreover, light radiates and can be perceived around people and things. And gazing at this soft glow of light, known as the aura, can open up a whole new sense of reality. As we respond to light, to electromagnetic fields, our eyes are stimulated, our moods are activated, our emotions are stirred. When this happens, the way in which we see others becomes more multi-dimensional. Various frequencies produce prismatic effects and these colors play off each other to produce visual magic, as if the soul itself is shimmering.

You can experiment with primary colors (red, yellow, and blue) and secondary colors (orange, green, and purple variations) to stimulate visual perceptual dynamics. Colors opposite each other on the spectrum are the easiest to work with. Place a bright orange on a cobalt-blue table cloth or some other large piece of cloth, and make sure there is good light all around it. Stare at the orange long enough to start relaxing, as if entering a trance. Then soften your stare into a daydreamy gaze. You will start to become aware of, and begin to see with, your peripheral vision. Keep gazing in a relaxed way until you see a glow of light around the orange. It will appear vibrant and electric. You may be able to discern bands of color within the spectrum of light surrounding the orange. This is the aura of the orange. You can see it. It is shimmering. It is fascinating and spiritually wondrous.

Now try this with people. Sit somewhere where you can observe another person. Focus all your attention on that person and gaze. This is easiest to do when the background is a blank, neutral, gray, or white. Soon you should be able to perceive a halo of light all around the person. It may appear white or silvery, or it may be a soft yellow or shimmer with other hues. There is no need to judge the colors and the effect of this light. Just enjoy it. You are not "on task" as you are normally expected to be, and that is okay. You are experimenting with your visual-perceptual sensing and it will be exciting for you. It may take time to ease into perceiving in this way. Remember to *gaze* as if in a daydream rather than *look* as if accomplishing a goal. The idea is to allow visual awareness of luminescence, to let your physical eyes perceive spiritually.

You will never see color in the same way again. You will never see people in the same way again, because you now realize they are imbued with light.

CHAPTER 8

TELEPATHIC COMMUNICATION

You do not have to be in close physical proximity to others to sense their energy empathically—either to feel their feelings or to realize that they feel yours. This is evident in our dream impressions or daydream wanderings, as well as in our spontaneous thoughts. This energy seems to flow easily, even when someone is half-way around the globe.

Empathic sensing involves connecting in a heart-centered way to our own energy and emotions as we open to the feelings of others. It occurs when we appreciate others and their ability to have an impact on us and our lives, and this can be felt whether they are near or far away.

When empaths think of someone, they often find that it is because that person is texting or emailing them at that very moment. There is a kind of invisible force of life that connects people, like strands of soul light flowing from one to another, a mutually sensed flow of energy. Because energy flows mysteriously in ways not subject to borders and boundaries, we can receive telepathic messages and we can send them. Sometimes they can arrive by surprise, effortlessly.

Special Delivery

One great way to develop empathic sensing is to experiment with intentionally sending telepathic messages. This requires a heart-centered focus that is finely tuned to the subtle fluctuations of energy that may flow in and out throughout the day. To direct this focus toward sending or receiving a specific message, allow silence more often and enter into the on-going empathic flow. This means that you must become aware of the fluctuations that stream in and around you. When you do, you are able to sense from the depths of your heart that you can send forth your feelings, your will-power, and your intentions and wishes to others.

Think of a specific person to whom you'd like to send a message. Concentrate on that person empathically. Recall the energy the person gives you, the feelings you get when he or she is near, and align with that energy. With all the force of that feeling, send the person the essence of yourself from your heart. Let your energy flow to the person based on the way his or her energy has enlivened you.

People often do this without having any idea they are doing so—perhaps because this type of energy work is not visible, only felt. It's like when we root for a team to win, projecting our wish for victory outward with the full unbridled force of our desire. Or when we are infatuated with someone and send out heartfelt empathic thoughts of love and admiration, willing the person to call or reach out. We humans love to get what we want. And when we send out these mental, emotional, psychological, and spiritual messages with the intention of bending others to our will, sometimes the results can seem just short of witchcraft. Often, we only get what we want long after we are no longer invested in the outcome. And trying to bend others to our will is, ultimately, manipulative and hazardous.

We also send out energy when we pray. In fact, prayer is simply the sending out of a spiritual plea, although it may feel more abstract to those who see God as largely conceptual. Prayer may feel different from sending a message out to a person, yet the power behind it is the same. When we pray, we send out the full force of our intention to have a loved one healed, or to get out of danger, or to make ourselves or someone else safe or fulfilled, and this has real resonance. In genuine prayer, we send out all we've got in us to realize what we think is best. And this is the same emotive energy that empowers empathic-psychic communication between two or more people. We send and receive empathic messages by noticing the subtle energies that are perceptible within our own being, and intentionally project those energies toward a focal point, a person, or a situation.

"My friend and I agreed to try to communicate psychically. So we set up a time and spent just a few minutes tuning in to each other. What I saw surprised me. It was a very striking image of a good witch standing in her living room. The witch had colorful hair and wore a blue velvet cape that she twirled to project energy that whipped around her. She said: 'Tell her to go ahead and buy kitchen utensils!' Turned out my friend was thinking of getting new kitchen gear, so this message was interesting.

My friend told me that she saw a wizard standing near me. He had a wand and a tall pointy hat with purple images on it, and a wide mischievous smile. He said: 'Just ask me for help, and it is yours.' Then she told me that she actually has small statues of a wizard and a witch on her mantelpiece. I told her that I have had wands in my dreams and keep seeing them in my life. This made us feel as if we had really connected telepathically."

Sending and Receiving

When sending and receiving empathic messages, it is best if you are relaxed, because the energy flows more smoothly when you are easy-going and not tensed up. Do not let doubtful thoughts enter your mind, like: "I must be wrong.

I am sure I am just making this up." Trust the flow and go with it all. Just note how you feel and consider whatever images you may see in your mind's eye—your third eye, your sixth sense. Remember, the imagination is very powerful. If you are exchanging messages with a willing partner, take turns so you can send while the other receives, and receive while the other is sending.

Here are a few simple ways in which you can experiment with sending and receiving empathic messages.

Cruise Control

We are often more psychic while in the car, spending time moving through space. This can also be true while riding a bike or walking. In fact, almost any physical motion that is relaxing can put you in a receptive mode. While you drive, don't think too hard. Try to get into a "cruise control" mode that makes you feel calm and allows you to be open to thoughts that randomly drift in and out. Take note of what passes through your mind. If you like, you can jot these impressions down after you've parked the car safely. You may want to keep a small journal in the glove compartment, because some thoughts and feelings you get while in a car can actually be pretty psychic. And sooner or later, these impressions may be validated.

"I was driving my three-year-old on an errand. From the back seat, he started telling me about when he had lived 'in the valley.' I was surprised that he even knew what a valley was, so I listened intently. He said: 'And they all told me not to go live in the valley because I wouldn't find a wife there.' I was shocked, because this was highly unusual talk for a three-year-old. So I said: 'What did you do in the valley?' He answered: 'I had gold that was all mine and I hid it. I had a mountain lion cub that I found and took care of.' This made me think of California and the Gold Rush, but there is no way he could know this. We lived in New England. Then I remembered that, before he was born, a Cherokee healer told me this child had been part of the Gold Rush in a past life. This all just amazed me."

Hide and Seek

If you have lost something and can't find it, ask a psychic buddy to connect with you empathically through a quick few minutes of meditation and see if the person can "find it." You can practice this skill, which is not unlike remote viewing, even when nothing is lost.

> "Sometimes I hide something and ask my sister, who lives several states away, to see if she can sense my energy and the energy in my home empathically. She can always tell me where the item is. I could even hide something like the tip of a pencil eraser and, somehow, she'd meditate and know where it was."

Long Distance Calls

Set a time with an empathic person who is willing to act as your supportive psychic buddy. Concentrate on each other for four to five minutes. Then share the thoughts or feelings you each receive. The images and emotions you receive may be either symbolic or literal.

Psychic Post Cards

Try sending a simple visual thought or message to some-one and see what happens. Pick a person you think will be willing to play with you. Send him or her a visual image of something easy and simple—a card from a regular deck, for example, like the Ace of Clubs, or an image of an animal. Spend time doing this throughout a day, then check back with your psychic buddy to see if the person got any images from you. And ask your buddy to send you a mental image as well.

Double Vision

Think of and imagine someone for four to five minutes, then ask the person to do the same, either before or after you. This will allow you to focus on receiving a message, and then allow the other person to focus on receiving a message from you in return. Surround the person with your energy. Imagine the person's energy. See the person as clearly as you can with your third eye. Take special note of any ran-dom thoughts or notions that come to you and write them down. Then ask the other person to do the same, without revealing what you received. Wait until the other person has meditated on you before you exchange and share.

> "I told my friend I'd concentrate on her and then see what images and thoughts I got. I instantly saw a car with an open hood. I could see all the parts and smell the grease. Then I saw her father, whom I had never met, drinking strong black cof-fee. When I told her this, she told me that her dad loved working on cars and drank his coffee black

with sugar, adding that, when he came home with his thermos, she'd get to drink some of his coffee. Then she told me that, when she concentrated on me, she saw rocking chairs and my mother watching us ride horses. We used to have black rocking chairs and my mother watched us ride horses from the kitchen window."

Yes or No

Tell your empathic psychic buddy that you are concentrating on a question that has a "yes" or "no" answer. This works best if the question has some genuine emotional impact. Ask your buddy to share a few moments of silence with you while you concentrate on your question, then ask whether the answer is "yes" or "no."

The Way of the Empath

Checking In

Try thinking of someone you have not heard from in a long while. Concentrate empathically on the person—how you feel about him or her, any memories or impressions of the person. Try sending the person loving thoughts or heartfelt energy. See what happens—you just may hear back!

> "I wanted to see what would happen if I concentrated on someone I have not heard from in a while to see if they'd contact me. So I focused on someone in my mind during meditation. I did the meditation a few times. Then my wife told me she received an email from that very person, so I was able to reply and explain how I had focused psychically to see if it would work—and it did!"

CHAPTER 9
EMPATHIC DRAWING

Drawing, especially free-style drawing done in the flowing stream of consciousness, offers an immediate mode of creative expression. This type of drawing accentuates empathic sensing, because it involves opening to feelings and expressing them in the gestural language of mark-making. Mark-making is innately compelling to humans because it allows us to make our own unique impression upon the world. Drawing on paper or on walls—or any other surface, for that matter—becomes symbolic of our agency to respond to life with vitality and personal empowerment. Drawing without self-criticism enables and frees the spirit within to do its magic in the world, whether we make those marks privately on a small scrap of paper, or with a finger in the snow, or in great public halls or thoroughfares.

As they mature, most people lose the natural impulse to draw with complete abandon as they once did when they were very young. The ability to draw freely what we feel in our hearts with a kind of wildly joyous release is often forgotten or devalued through conditioning as we grow older. It is worth recapturing that ingenuity and spontaneity, however, because, by doing so, we reclaim our freedom of expression and our exuberance. When we make marks with utter joy like toddlers, we engage in an outpouring of feeling that, coupled with the self-assertion of changing a surface by freely marking on it, is very empowering. And it is a good empathic creative process to recapture. Emotions expressed and transformed into visual images are exciting; they reaffirm our nature as born creators. Mark-making as an empathic expression can encourage deeper empathic sensing and embolden the creator to embrace a momentous wave of emotion and do something interesting with it.

Stream Drawing

You can reclaim your intuitive, creative genius by following the simple steps laid out in my book *Making Marks: Discover the Art of Intuitive Drawing* (Atria Books, 2014). The key to this kind of drawing, called stream drawing, is to approach the process without self-criticism, without feeling that you have to make a "good drawing." This lets you draw and then reflect on the marks you make, opening your mind and heart to a personal intuitive conversation that can heighten your awareness and bring you interesting insights.

For the purposes of this book, we will use stream drawing to enter an imaginary realm within. Through it, we will achieve an unhindered stream of consciousness and a meditative state that will liberate your agency as creator using your innate urge to make marks.

Start by removing the general obstacles that impede your empathically charged creative motions—your own self-protectiveness. Unfortunately, our society has taught us that drawing is not particularly useful or important and that art must be representational or largely used for commercial purposes like advertising. So it is reasonable that we have become inhibited by this conditioning and these expectations, and that we are reticent and cautious when we commit ourselves to putting marks on paper. We fear we will be made to feel vulnerable or ashamed.

To recapture the spirit of creative mark-making, try closing your eyes when you draw, so you can focus more on how it feels to draw, on the sensual quality of drawing, on how it feels to pour out your emotions through mark-making. This requires an open and bold understanding that drawing is not just for creating an image or rendering a specific form. Rather the act of drawing itself is an *empathic* activity whose point is the process, not the result. By closing your eyes while you draw, you allow yourself to enter a very sensual creative-meditative state that is intensely evocative, emotive, and enjoyable. It is also very easy to do.

There is no right or wrong way to draw freely. The following steps just set you up to be able to draw without self-consciousness. Here's what you'll need:

- Some blank pieces of paper, at least 8"x10"

- A sharp pencil (pencils usually feel better than pens)

- A comfortable place to sit with a nice surface on which to work (just a table and chair will do)

With pencil in hand and paper ready, close your eyes and follow these four steps:

- *Draw with Emotion.* Allow your heart to open and to fill you with an anticipation of creating freely. Begin drawing one continuous line that moves all over the paper in loops or zig-zags or waves or whatever you feel like doing. Keep your pencil on the paper, imagining it to be like a skater gliding all over a large frozen pond. Don't lift your pencil, because, if you do, you will most likely hesitate and open your eyes. This will take you out of the flowing meditative stream of consciousness and possibly even cause you to feel self-critical. Note the tactile sensation you feel while drawing. Try applying different kinds of pressure, perhaps changing from bearing down heavily to skimming lightly over the surface. Listen to how the pencil sounds on the paper and go with how it feels. Is there a lot of tension in your hand as you grip the pencil or are you relaxed?

- *Gaze.* Now open your eyes and "gaze" at what you drew, seeing without imposing conditions or judgment. Look at your drawing as if you are in a day-

dream that began when you closed your eyes. Using a soft gaze, pay attention to how you feel as you explore the visual imagery. Does it look the way you imagined it might? Do you see shapes that your mind wants to identify? Do you see anything recognizable? Do you feel that the lines you drew convey emotion or persuasions? As you look at the drawing you made, breathe it all in. Encompass the entire drawing as an expression of your uniqueness; appreciate what just happened.

- *Trust What Comes.* If you think random thoughts while gazing at the drawing, trust them, even if they don't seem to have a rational reason for entering your mind. Write them down below or to the side of the drawing. If you feel specific emotions or have memories triggered or thoughts spring up in direct relation to the lines, write them down as well. For instance: "I see a long swoop moving up and it feels exciting, like being on a roller coaster." Or: "I see a jagged gash that feels like anger or a warning of some kind." Don't label the marks you made as loops or circles or straight lines. Just describe them as feelings and associations or memories that arise as a result of gazing at the lines you drew.

- *Reflect and Connect.* After you have written down all that flowed into your thoughts and feelings while gazing, consider the notes you made in a deeper empathic way. For example, let's say you saw a cup in your drawing and jotted down "tea cup." Now go beyond labeling the image and dig beneath the surface of what "tea cup" signifies for you. Write down any feelings you may have associated with tea or tea cups or tea-drinking. Notice any memories you may have in relation to tea cups. Memories often hold many feelings and unresolved emotional conflicts or wounds that are waiting for a chance to be expressed and resolved through a creative-intuitive process.

Here's an example of how memories may arise. Your first memory may be that you have some fancy tea cups that you only use for special occasions. Then, going deeper, you may add that you have not even been able to have anyone over for tea in ages, which makes you feel like getting ready to invite people over again. Also, these cups were a gift from your ex-partner and you have mixed emotions about them. The solution you write might go like this: "I see that being reminded of tea cups is loaded. It makes me sad, but optimistic and ultimately grateful, because they're so nice. And it shows me that, although they are a weird reminder of the past, I am going to enjoy using them because I like them."

This kind of empathic mark-making can expand in ways that are truly wonderful and unexpected, synchronistic

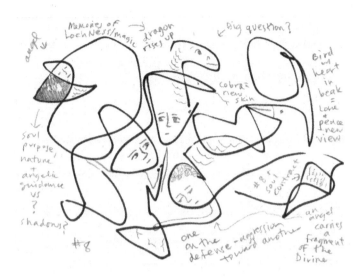

and healing. You can stream draw with a particular concern you have in mind, asking to receive spiritual guidance from the marks you make with your eyes closed. And during the gazing and trusting process, you may discover some interesting answers, solutions, and ideas that you can apply to your concern. Here is an example of the stream drawing described above after gazing, trusting, and reflecting.

Blind Contour Drawing

This drawing practice is an excellent way to build empathic sensing. Artists draw empathically as a rule, since marks graphically communicate emotion. They know that to draw loosely and freely is key, since no drawing feels good to look at if it did not feel good to draw. When artists render a person or an object, therefore, they focus intensely on the subject of the drawing. They let go of self-criticism completely and get lost in an empathic experience, diving deeply into the feelings of the subject—the person, place, or thing they are drawing. The lines they draw transfer the feelings of the subject as perceived by the artist, directly onto the paper.

The whole point of artistic creation is, in fact, to enter an authentically empathic creative space, and to capture and convey the feeling and presence of life beheld in the subject. A bottle may have all kinds of emotional expressiveness in its shape, or a person may be suggestive of a range of emotions like sorrow or haughtiness, depending on the pose of the body itself. The attitude conveyed by the subject is what the artist seeks to capture. But this cannot happen if the mark-maker is looking at the drawing rather than concentrating on the subject. When this happens, creators miss out on a robust empathic connection between themselves and their subject.

Blind contour drawing is similar to stream drawing in that you cannot see what you are drawing. And this is good. Why? Because it forces you to be so focused on what or whom you are drawing that the contour line you create (the outline of the object or the person's body) is the result of your inner sensing, not your eyes. As you feel your way along the surface of the contour, you draw as if you are experiencing it, feeling every curve, capturing every expressive angle with one continuous line.

Here's what you'll need:

- White paper, at least 8"x10." Larger is better, perhaps a newsprint pad.

- Pencil or charcoal. Pencils are great for this, as is very fine and delicate vine charcoal.

- An object to draw, like a vase or a branch from a tree. Start with an object and then move on to people or animals.

- A clear surface on which to draw. You can use a table, but you will have to keep yourself from looking down at your drawing while you work. Standing at an easel is preferable, because you will not be as tempted to look down to see what you are drawing.

Remember: If you see what you are drawing, you risk breaking the trance-like flow of stream of consciousness. Self-consciousness interrupts the flow and causes you to focus more on your drawing and less on your subject. The first contour drawing below was made of a pair of scissors, rendered multiple times on the same sheet of paper. The second was made of a pair of reading glasses rendered multiple times on the same sheet of paper.

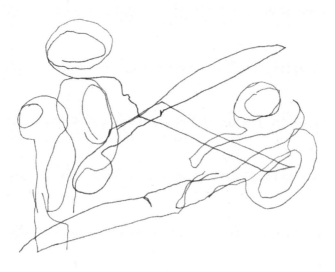

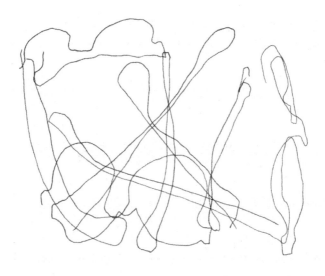

Drawing Buddies

When doing empathic drawing, stream drawing, or contour drawing (or any other type of empathic drawing you may discover or invent), it is really nice to have a trusted friend—someone who will be your empathic psychic buddy—to share the experience. You and your buddy can practice "seeing into" situations empathically and offering different perspectives. This buddy should be someone you trust, someone with whom you enjoy partnering, someone with whom you can have fun working on creative projects.

When you stream draw for someone else, you simply dedicate your own stream drawing to that person without knowing their concerns. Then you describe what you see in the drawing as a way of offering support for whatever those concerns are. This is not done in the spirit of "revealing" something or exploiting someone else's feelings, but rather as a sharing of what is internal for you (and therefore about you). It can help you understand that, in our shared experience as humans, we are connected by symbolic signs we perceive to reach clarity.

Stream drawings are multi-dimensional and can be literal. But they can also be a way to acknowledge what you see and feel based on the imagery drawn. They should never be used as a means to analyze another (or another's drawing), but rather as a way to impart the thoughts and feelings you get from *your own stream drawing* done in that person's honor. This can allow you to join together to offer support and discover empathic synchronicities that may hold real meaning for you both.

"I had a decision to make about whether to get involved with a project and I felt uncomfortable about it. So I asked my friend to help me figure it out empathically. I concentrated on whether or not my intuitive take was something I should trust and closed my eyes and did a stream drawing. I shared it with my friend and we both saw a big rat right in the center of the drawing and decided maybe I was right not to trust the situation, that I should trust myself more. I declined getting involved in the project and felt much better. The stream drawing really helped and having another intuitive take on it was great."

CHAPTER 10
DREAM-HELPER CIRCLES

Some contemporary empaths have had a very impressive impact on our cultural attitude toward consciousness, empathic sensing, and intuitive knowing. Henry Reed is one of these. Reed has done exciting experimental work that has earned him recognition as the Father of the Dream Movement. His ground-breaking use of dreaming to gain intuitive, empathic insight and connectedness with others has established intuitive knowing as a force that connects us, rather than separates us. "What is significant to our investigations," Reed claims, "is that during such communication, there is no sense of separation between perceiver and perceived, unlike 'objective' intuition, which involves a separation between subject and object."

The beauty of Reed's work is that it is centered in the expansion of empathy for others, as the intention to connect empathically with others simultaneously creates more self-awareness. Partners join together, opening intuitively to one another, *for the other as self.* In this process, intuitive impressions arrive as a benefit to the partner as much as for a deeper understanding of the self. Since perceivers remain unaware of the specifics of the target focus, Reed explains, the intuitive impressions are shared and both the perceivers and the focus person work together to see the way in which they and we are innately connected.

As director of the Edgar Cayce Institute for Intuitive Studies, Reed dedicated his life's work to creating and advocating for an applied spiritual science of intuition based in the life and work of Edgar Casey. His progressive studies and experiments have had an enormous impact on an increasingly open cultural acceptance of psychic phenomenon. His experimentation has had fascinating and transformational results for participants, providing credible and meaningful evidence that empathic, intuitive, and imaginative processes create meaningful synchronicities and astounding opportunities for conscious awareness. His work has brought us closer to an acknowledgment that open-hearted empathy is a necessary element in any truly functional and compassionate society.

Reed developed what he called "the dream-helper circle," a kind of social dreamwork based in a transpersonal and intuitively dynamic process. One such circle, brought together during a retreat in Virgina, consisted of about a dozen participants who were unknown to each other. One participant volunteered to be the focus person, while the others agreed to dream about her. Nobody knew the issues or concerns of this volunteer, but all agreed to dedicate their dreams to her, to her well-being, and to helping solve her problem and heal her distress.

The circle gathered around the volunteer and together spoke a ritualistically meaningful affirmation: "I promise to remember a dream for you tonight." That night, the participants all went to sleep, ready to see what dreams would come on behalf of the volunteer. They committed to writing down any scenes, feelings, fragments, or dream impressions they received on awakening.

The next morning, everyone gathered to share the dreams they had had throughout the night. One at a time, they described their dreams and were astonished to find they had very similar themes and imagery. Most had to do with the uneasiness of transitions, with moving belongings like furniture, with staying out of inclement weather, and with various archetypal threads of imagery and suggestions around the topic of being married or not being married.

After everyone had shared the details of their dreams, elaborating on the accompanying emotions present in them, the focus person disclosed her concerns. The issue she hoped to resolve had to do with whether or not she should remain in her marriage, and how all the details weighed on her— where to live, what would need to be moved and changed if she moved out, how to build a new life outside of the marriage. It became clear to everyone who had participated that, simply by stating their intention to dedicate a dream to the focus person, they had validated her concerns, received appropriate answers, and given her support. Each dreamer then reflected on the patterns in their own dreams, as well as the dreams of the other participants, looking for the personal meaning within them. Clearly the messages and guidance in their dream impressions had served both them and the woman who volunteered to be the focus person.

Intuitive Hearts

The utter beauty of this empathic endeavor is that it demonstrates that, together, we are able to perceive messages that support others as they seek to resolve life's questions and challenges. Unlike any other empathic process,

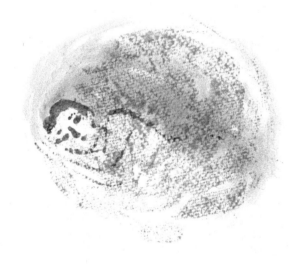

dream-helper circles address an individual's specific life challenges while affirming that, in our personal and communal pursuit of healing, we are all essentially interconnected and empowered to transcend our human conditions. As we offer our empathic sensing to benefit others, through dreams or otherwise, we are in turn able to see how our impressions and empathic sensing simultaneously guide us as well.

Reed's book, *Night and Day: Use the Power of Your Dreams to Transform Your Life* (2001), as well as his many other books and scholarly articles, have opened our culture to accept heart-centered intuitive exploration and expanded our understanding of the importance of empathic sensing through dreams and through partnering together for insight. His work unveils the many ways we can be enlightened, from our innermost intuitive hearts. Through Reed's inventive empathic approaches, we have come to recognize that empathic sensing and subconscious dream impressions offer far more than had previously or commonly been assumed. Dreams, he has assured us, are not strictly tools for mental-health diagnosis or maps for analyzing mental states. Rather they are something intrinsically and spiritually more.

Dreams are the place where we all meet through signs, symbols, and archetypal imagery, as well as through thought and feeling. Dreams bring enlightenment for us as dreamers, as well as for those for whom we may dream. When we dream together, we reach new heights of clarity and dreaming becomes the new, wild frontier of conscious emanations shared.

We are shifting collectively in the direction of understanding empathic sensing and psychic phenomenon. As we do so, a vastly exciting and enlightening opportunity is opening before us as we become increasingly able to explore transcendental methods. Reed's ingenious work leaves a great legacy for empaths and for anyone interested in empathic sensing, connecting, and living.

CHAPTER 11
SELF-PROTECTION

Living as a sensitive is not unlike Little Red Riding Hood skipping through a dark forest where wolves lurk. In fact, empaths need protection, because they are more susceptible than others. Therefore, they have to be even more conscientious than most in developing self-protective coping skills.

One immediate way empaths know when they are in danger is when they feel it internally. Warning messages may come into their awareness as thoughts or emotions, or by the way their stomachs or other energy centers feel. But they may not honor these inner messages of precaution. And when they ignore this inner guidance, empaths can get hurt.

It makes perfect sense that the process of self-protection for empaths starts from within. Following are two strategies that empaths can—and must—use to protect themselves.

R-E-S-P-E-C-T

Just as the song by Otis Redding, magnificently performed by Aretha Franklin, reminds us, respect is mandatory. As we read in the first chapter, self-love, self-forgiveness, and self-respect are essential for positive outcomes. And yet, people may at times injure themselves through self-sabotage that may be unconscious.

Self-respect does not mean selfishness, or feeling supremely entitled, or arrogance. It does not mean trashing others—which usually only causes those doing the trashing to get trashed themselves. It means valuing the worth of the self, and honoring the self (and others) enough to keep destructive patterns and abusive situations from developing.

Unconditional Love

Unconditional love is a perplexing concept—one that may be more of a theory than a practice for humans, it seems. People have a very hard time feeling love for those who cross boundaries, or engage in emotional or material theft, or are completely lacking in empathy. Yet empaths go into sentient trances when encountering others—perhaps reaching out to pristine souls who may have been damaged early in life, perhaps connecting with others who have made terrible choices, perhaps risking contact with others who are dangerous to those around them.

Because of this kind of empathic exposure, empaths learn through time and painful experience that they do not need to take responsibility for others. Empaths feel best when avoiding toxic relationships, jobs, and places, even if they feel an outpouring of love for a person involved, or a strong inner conflict about the situation. They learn that it is possible to feel unconditional love while maintaining good boundaries.

> "My friend did not want me to idealize potential romantic partners. I told her I don't idealize potential romantic partners; I idealize everyone."

Falling in love with what is fascinating, beautiful, and interesting about an individual is not a bad thing. Appreciation of others is very life-enhancing, inclusive, and idealistic for many empaths. Seeing "the good" in someone as opposed to focusing on "the bad" is a positive gesture from the heart. However, ignoring human nature and losing the self when connecting with others is detrimental for empaths.

When we idealize others, we, in a way, objectify them. We are often more "in love" with our idea of others than we are committed to learning how to respond to who they really are—who they are choosing to be, how they are prioritizing their lives. It helps to evaluate ourselves when appreciating others, perhaps asking: "Am I loving this person or my projection of who this person is?" Loving the soul essence of someone requires no designs or conditions. Unconditional love for others brings on a rush of compassion for them, recognizing their unique spiritual presence beneath both their personality and their physicality.

Dangerous Liasons

One of the hardest things for empaths to do is to relate to people who are not particularly empathic, who don't show much empathy, or who have a low tolerance for those who do. And, of course, empaths are easily drawn to such people! Sometimes they sense an injury in someone who lacks empathy and want to help heal the injury. People are complex; they are like shimmering mosaics of complicated traits and experiences. And they often possess so many admirable qualities that it can be difficult to recognize or pay attention to signs of emotional danger, like a lack of feeling for others or an inability to return love. Empaths are often caught in adoring relationships with others, mistaking them as mutually sensitive, only to find out too late that the entire construct of their bond was illusory.

Here are some tips on how to avoid these hazards.

Observe

When empaths approach others with an open heart and are spoken to insensitively, this is distressing. The good news is that you can choose not to approach or seek out others who greet you with a cold affronting response, and you can try not to use those phrases you find hurtful when talking with others. Here are a few phrases that empaths may find toxic:

- Lighten up!
- Oh, you are just imagining it.
- Stop being so paranoid.
- Don't bleed all over everyone.
- I hate the way you cry so easily.
- You're too nice.
- Don't take everything so personally.
- I was just playing devil's advocate.

Sometimes people enjoy setting up empaths by asking them how they feel, only to dismiss them after they've given a sincere answer. Again, this is a situation in which you will want to pay attention. Be wise about those with whom you share, as not all interactions are productive. This extends to greater questions as well, like whether or not its constructive to be closely connected with someone, or live with someone, or be married to someone. You may find yourself very close to others who are injurious to you. Through life experience, you will come to know what situations are best for you and which are destructive to you as you develop your empathic sensing and intuitive knowing.

Judge Situations, Not People

We often learn most from relationships that are difficult, messy, and painful. And these are unavoidable. The good news is that you can decide through those experiences what you prefer and what you dislike, what makes you uncomfortable, what you want to change about yourself, and how to choose more wisely going forward.

As you seek protection from what may be damaging to you, however, there is no need to judge others. Rather, judge *situations* that may be unhealthy in your relationship dynamics. Empathic wellness includes having a sense of purpose. And you are the author of your own life story. You determine where you allow yourself to go and with whom you engage and connect. It is essential that you exercise your own agency in making choices and in dealing with consequences. But you can do this without judging others. The key is to focus on the situations a person may bring into your life, and discern which situations are healthy for you. Then you can choose to allow them or not, which may mean moving on from some relationships.

Here are some questions you can ask yourself when confronted with situations that require choice and discernment:

- Do the situations I'm in due to this relationship feel good to me?

- Do these situations enhance my ability to be genuinely myself?

- Do situations with this person help me deepen my sense of love?

- How do I feel intrinsically about the situations this relationship entails?

- What sensations do I feel in my body when I am in a situation with this person?

- Am I able to function fully with strength, or do these situations leave me feeling drained and weak?

The Dominion of Self

As an empathic person, consider yourself a *place*. You are a universe unto yourself, like a planet with an energetic ecosystem and a fluctuating emotional, mental, spiritual, and physical climate. You experience peaks and valleys and have rivers streaming through your body. Meridian lines of energy flow beneath your skin. Atmospheric conditions are influenced by the energy centers of your body. There is a direct connection between your emotional or mental state and your physical response to it.

Now and then, your energy may be blocked and this can be felt in various ways. For example, a situation you're in may create tension in your stomach or neck. As your muscles tighten up, the flow of energy in your body is affected and pain results. Inflammation may even build in that area that requires attention for healing.

Empaths feel tension easily, so it is important that you listen to your physical response system. Because you viscerally sense and feel energy coming at you throughout the day and it all gets internalized, it is important to become more conscious of why you are feeling certain sensations. Clearing your own vibrational fields is equally essential as you contemplate what stirs in you that makes you uncomfortable or what stands out in a positive way. Release what is not optimal or healthy to remain strong. Honor your energetic space, both inside and out.

Call Up the Color Guard

Around every person's body there is a magnificent field of energy, a radiant aura that surrounds them with a layer of mixed energies. You can see it in color, through aura-gazing. It contains the person's current mood as well as the purity of his or her soul beyond the personality. In fact, each person radiates a small cosmos of mental, physical, emotional, and spiritual energies that can have a big impact on the immediate environment and on others in the vicinity.

Sometimes, the entire ecology of a room changes when a single person enters—like a wind blowing across the plains that suddenly refreshes atmospheric conditions. The room may seem to grow colder or become electrified. It may suddenly seem to be brimming with giddiness or even have a warm brilliance. Sometimes that energy may seem frightful or shadowy, repellent. Sometimes a person may look very appealing and be immensely charming, but have an energy field that does not feel good to you.

Often external visuals like beauty can obscure what is in the energy field. Or someone who is not strikingly attractive may be dismissed, even though that person has wonderful energy. In the case of negative energy hiding beneath a pretty facade, you may sense this, register it, and be charmed by it, but will probably not be able to ignore the negative vibes you are picking up. At other times, someone's energy may be so filled with excitement, charisma, and magnetism that everyone wants to bathe in it and gravitate toward it, letting their own magnetic fields blend with it. In fact, that is what happens when you encounter others; you soak yourself in their energy.

Avoid Energy Vampires

People feed off the energy of others—and empaths taste good! When a group of friends gets together because they are alike, they often get bored (unconsciously) with the generally similar energy exchanged between them and seek out others who can bring a different vibration into the group. At times, that different energy may come from empaths, because they are so open to others and may not suspect that they are about to be devoured.

But empaths get involved with people who are not "like them"—at times, to their detriment. And once they realize that they are not valued or appreciated, yet are still pursued by those who may not treat them well, they have to remain steadfast and get comfortable with the uncomfortableness of being unavailable.

When you find yourself pursued by "vampires" who want to suck the energy out of you, be prepared and unafraid to stand up for yourself. You can be kind, yet still keep your distance. You can avoid giving away personal details that an energy vampire may use against you. You can be benevolently well-wishing without being available. People may punish you when you pull back to protect yourself because, remember, they are being fed by the energy they are siphoning off. So even if it feels socially unpleasant, it is crucial to create boundaries.

Eventually, you will develop skills to help you circumnavigate energy-suckers and be able to go back to cultivating an inner garden of peace that you will see reflected outwardly in your immediate environment and in the enjoyment of true friends. You will also develop the ability to discern by paying attention to what you feel around others and by remaining unavailable to what does not feel

good—period. It is better to be alone or to have just one true friend than to have precious life energy drained away by hungry opportunists.

Empaths don't need to rush to answer everyone's calls or meet everyone's demands for their attention. Because they tend to be so open, willing, and accommodating, *acquiring the skill of conscious responding is paramount.* You can give yourself permission to wait, to reflect, and to respond more slowly, on your own schedule. If others truly wish to be friends, they will understand and be supportive, even after long absences. True companions are eager to hear how their friends are and it will seem as if no time has passed once you do reconnect.

Be Real

For many, the best form of protection comes through spoken or sung prayer or affirmations. These can be very

powerful when voiced from the heart and mind with real
sincerity. All cultures have forms of wisdom for aligning
with a sense of wholeness in our relationships.

The truth often gets obscured in relationships, but it
is best to stay in touch with your inner truths. When you
stay steadfast in your own truth and are unafraid to speak
it out loud, manipulators and those with hidden agendas
or a desire to suck up your energy will quickly move on—
unless they think they can wear you down eventually. Try
it and see. Some may continue to attempt to break down
your resolve, and that alone is a big red flag. Watch what
people do in response when you exhibit self-respect. What
do you see? The great Chief Seattle once said: "Show up,
pay attention, tell the truth." He knew that if you show up
(be responsible), pay attention (really notice how you feel
and what you observe), and tell the truth (be outspoken
and unafraid to be yourself), you will eventually reach the
summit of the human spirit.

Be Clear

Many cultures have traditional ways of clearing the energy
of the places they inhabit. Some use salt or sage, believ-
ing that the tiny crystals and the rising smoke send energy
up to the Great Spirit. Others use holy water blessed by
a cleric or a spiritual teacher. Some use crystals to bring
clearing energy into a space. And the words said during
cleansing rituals can act as important statements of intention and ownership of the energy in a space, indicating
what is allowed and what is not.

However you choose to clear and clean your energetic environment, you can give your actions potency by

including some form of physical gesture in your ritual. Some rock back and forth; some kneel; some make the sign of the cross; some light a candle. All are powerful and effective practices when sincerely felt. When you incorporate fine and large motor skills into your prayers to set your intentions for protection and change, you ensure that your words are felt in both body and soul.

Salt can also be used to clear the auric field, so a salt bath or a plunge into salty seawater is good for empaths. Even walking along a shoreline breathing in salty sea air is good for clearing the aura.

Be Balanced

One way for empaths to protect themselves is to learn about the energy centers of the body called "chakras." The seven chakras are like spinning spirals of energy that lie along the spine from crown to root. They whirl constantly based on your moods, your physical state, and your emotional and mental conditions. Chakras churn with spiritual, soul energy that works within your physical being as you experience corporeal life.

In Hindu tradition, the chakras support our spiritual orientation within the physical body and align us to what is sacred—to third-eye vision, to self-expression, to emotions and love, to harmony and safety, to creative powers and primal urges. When empaths knowingly harmonize with these centers, it creates a kind of firewall that maintains their authority over the dominion of the self.

Keeping the chakras in balance is invaluable for empaths, whether through yoga, pranic healing modalities, or Reiki, an ancient Japanese healing art. Being consciously aware of these centers and meditating on them helps keep those who absorb empathic energy feeling their best. Empaths' chakras are often wide open because they think they have to make others happy, and this can lead to exhaustion and disharmony within the chakra system.

The spiritual energy of the chakras is enlivening when balanced—when each chakra is in harmonious relation to the others—and you project this vibrancy and balance out into world. When the chakras are out of balance—when one energy center struggles, for example—you may feel drained, weak, nervous, or heavy-hearted. This is why it is so important that you avoid seeking validation "out there," and rather attune to what is happening "in here." You can do this by cultivating a conscious awareness of the chakras and connecting with them through meditation.

Here is a list of the seven chakras and an example of how each affects you when out of balance:

- *Crown chakra.* "I feel light headed." "I'm under so much pressure, my head hurts."

- *Third-eye chakra.* "I'm so upset I can't see straight." "Everything looks so rosy to me."

- *Throat chakra.* "My throat is constricting." "I feel like singing, I'm so happy."

- *Heart chakra.* "My heart is crushed." "I am so light-hearted."

- *Solar-plexus chakra.* "I feel butterflies in my stomach." "I have the heaviest feeling at the pit of my stomach."

- *Sacral chakra.* "I am so bored." "I have the best ideas today."

- *Root chakra.* "I want it so badly my legs tremble." "I feel so at home here."

Be Grounded

Because empaths are so sensitive to energy, they may spend the first portion of a long life feeling ungrounded, as if they are about to float off into outer space. As observers,

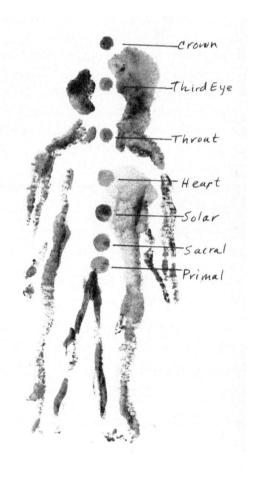

empaths are ethereally present and watching, while most others seem to be *in* the game rather than observing it.

It may upset you when you feel invalidated because others may not pick up on the vibrations or ribbons of information that are apparent to you, and this can create nervousness until you learn to trust yourself in spite of what others see or do not see and sense. These feelings often derive from a lack of self-esteem that can take time to work out. But you will become more foundationally present or settled as you manage (and celebrate) your heightened sensitivities.

Moody Blues

The extra load of feelings that empaths carry around puts a lot of strain on them, and this can lead to anxiety, self-consciousness, and depression. This, in turn, can leave intelligent, empathic, sensitive, and compassionate people thinking there is something wrong with them. After all, why do they so often feel nervous, unsure of themselves, and drained?

As an empath, you have brilliant extra-sensory abilities, and because these are not often recognized or acknowledged, you may feel anxious or inadequate. But you need protection and healthy boundaries to function well and with confidence, so you need to devise ways to block negative energy that is destructive.

Dome of Light

You can protect against unwanted attention by using imaginal-spiritual techniques like envisioning a field of white light energy around your body. Place it there by the power of creative visualization; make it be so! Sense what the light feels like as it surrounds you wherever you go. Imagine you are covered with pure white light that repels negative energies and blasts anyone who approaches with blazing light-filled energy. Feel the light; picture it fully surrounding you.

When anyone approaches you or enters your personal space, see this light buffering their energy. Focus on extending this dome of light from head to toe, keeping you safe. This alone will slow down your responses and keep you from reacting impulsively to others even when you aren't safe emotionally, mentally, physically, or spiritually. This dome of light can shelter you and give you time to be fully present within your own embodiment. It can also light up others while simultaneously protecting you.

Space Bender

Imagine the space between you and others—what artists call negative space—full of light, spirit guides, and angelic protectors who are there to align you with the people with whom you need to connect. Let them protect you from situations that may not best serve you as an empathic person. As your aura lights you up, your energy fills this negative space and your simplest gestures send beams forth that signal your intentions, your actions, and your choices to the wider world.

Meditate on visualizing this projection of your energy and the energy between people and objects so that it becomes routine as you go about your day-to-day activities. This supports your higher self as a witness to your physical self and gives you a spiritual perspective, a more consciously present disposition. And don't forget that, because you are a creator made in the image of the Great Creator, what you envision is not just imaginary. It is yours as you make it be so as an intention.

Beware Social Medea

Protection for empaths today must include barriers against exposure on more levels than just normal human face-to-face encounters. Today, empaths must deal with social media as well. Like Medea in the Greek myth, social media has the power to enhance life, but also has the ability to take it. In some ways, it is killing our collective innocence and does, in many ways, directly harm our children.

Social media has so much good in it. It abounds in useful information and enables communication between loved ones that takes place in the blink of an eye. Great things can be accomplished when using it as a platform to build awareness of a just cause, or raise money for someone in dire need after a tragedy, or activate conversations between those who may never have come into contact otherwise. It is creating a global community through the revolutionary technology of the internet.

But it has also created an environment in which self-expression is mocked, cruelty and aggression are facilitated, and self-absorbed, narcissistic tendencies are encouraged. People generate negative content designed to maim and bring about destruction and exploitation. Social media platforms create facades and illusions. And that falsity has become our mode of connection. Empaths need to understand the effect this can have on themselves and others.

And it's not only the content on social media that can be highly toxic to empaths. Just using the computer itself can be a challenge. Many empaths describe having trouble with computers, as if the energy of the internet clashes with their own sensitive energy.

Change the Channel

Most empaths report that movie scenes have a real effect on them, because they feel the intense drama of pain, fear, and torment so viscerally. Although they know a story may be fiction, they feel its emotional or mental or psychological message and frequency as if it were real.

> "In freshman year of high school, I saw a movie in which Peter Fonda's character dies at the end on his motorcycle. I was so disturbed by it that I got upset. My friends said: 'Oh, it's just a movie.' But for me, it was really upsetting."

For empaths, there is no shrugging off violence in the media as "just a movie." So choosing to "change the channel" when exposed to disturbing psychological thrillers, scenes of torture, and images of abuse or murder is highly beneficial.

Because, as an empath, great emotion will swell and remain within you, keeping that toxic and hostile energy to a minimum and processing it through creativity or prayer and meditation is best for you. When you are exposed to violence—even fictional violence—you may feel drenched inside and out with distress, because these depictions fill you up like putrid water poured into a clean vessel. And unpleasing visual imagery can be poisonous.

Be My Hero

The victim/rescuer archetype is a familiar one to empaths because, although they routinely feel victimized as they navigate in a somewhat brutal world, they also have a simultaneous desire to rescue others from pain.

This means that many empaths get entangled in relationships grounded in the victim/rescuer archetype, both attributes being continually juggled between both partners. Whose turn is it to need rescuing? Whose turn is it to come to the rescue? Whose turn is it to feel victimized again? This is something you may grow out of with conscious awareness as life plays out for you.

Please note: This dynamic can be extreme and become tragic. If you are in any way physically or emotionally harmed, your first priority is to remove yourself from danger. This is sometimes easier said than done, but staying where you may encounter abuse is not sustainable.

CHAPTER 12

EMPATHS IN THE WORLD TODAY

Empathic people are found in every profession, even in the most unlikely places. Even an accountant, who is arguably more fixated on numbers than on people's feelings, may be heard to claim he is "a real people person." But all occupations are enhanced and made more bearable when those gifted with empathic knowing and awareness are present, because empaths want to exist in a climate of compassion and have a strong desire to help others feel valued.

Certainly, businesses, enterprises, schools, community systems, and organizations that lack empathy can be scary places. Exploitation comes easily in situations where there is a distorted frame of reference toward people, whether they are employees, students, colleagues, clients, or volunteers. Warped and exploitative practices arise when people feel a lack of empathy. We all feel it when things seem unfair.

Empaths can be found in a wide variety of roles, but it is not easy for them to be in situations where they feel self-protective or drained of their energy, where they regularly hear cynical words or must deal with highly aggressive environments. Since competition for empaths is not as healthy as cooperation, they do best when focusing on jobs that heal others, bring enlightenment, or ease suffering for many or for a select few. Here are some life paths that have proven to be healthy for empaths:

- Alternative-healing practitioners

- Medical practitioners

- Teachers

- Therapists

- Visual artists

- Musicians

- Poets and writers

- Spiritual scholars and leaders

- Firefighters
- Hospice workers
- Non-profit workers

Help Wanted

So how do empaths cope with a lack of empathy in others and in organizations? Sometimes enduring a less-than-ideal situation forces them to build inner structures of protection. But ultimately, empaths are better off when they are in a space that resonates with their personal vision and ideology. Here are some ways you can create and find refuge in those spaces.

Walk On By

Empaths do well where they can thrive and live life the way they'd most like to experience it. They are most comfortable when they are able to be themselves openly. We've all been in uncomfortable situations that we felt we couldn't improve. When you decide you cannot make a place or situation better, you may need to find your way into your own kind of setting—whether that be a school, a job, or a neighborhood. Sometimes making a quick exit and moving on to something more suitable is the best strategy.

Meditate, Envision

Empaths are very sensitive to the spaces they enter. Try using meditation and creative visualization to help you find a space in which you can thrive and where you can realize new opportunities. Being patient and consistently envisioning open doors, fortuitous chance meetings, and advantageous encounters can help you find a true vibrational match.

Get Involved

While activism is necessary and important to bring about solutions for governments and societies, you may feel less inclined to take to the streets in protest and be more drawn to quiet forms of activism. You may be more comfortable generating creative energy away from the crowds, doing your part by personally working to enhance others' lives through service.

Try turning to creative pursuits through which you can influence norms by introducing new ideas. Look for occupations that allow you to communicate empathy through creative expression, engagement, and volunteerism. You will be at your best and accomplish the most change when you operate from the heart—from the core, from the inside out. When you use your unique talents to the fullest, expressing your own convictions in your own voice, you can activate meaningful connection on your own terms. Service toward others can manifest as small kind gestures or quietly acknowledging others—which can often have the greatest impact anyway.

Follow Your Inner Compass

If you feel a situation is repugnant or corrupt in some way, you may not be able to change the structure or the people functioning within it, and you may feel guilty for trying to extract yourself from it. You may tend to think more about what is best for others—the boss, colleagues, etc.—than about what is best for you. You even may feel uncomfortable thinking that your departure or your reasons for going may hurt others' feelings.

This is especially true in situations where children are involved—in a school setting, for example. You may find it hard to move on if you realize that children will still be subjected to what you find unacceptable. But if doing all you can does not rectify the situation, go where your inner compass leads you, although you may devise ways to have a positive impact on individuals you care about once you've moved on.

> "I once saw a first grader refusing to cooperate with a security officer, lying on the floor and refusing to move. The kid was a 'runner,' a child who takes off from the classroom without permission. In the interaction with the security guard, I could see that he could not get out of the situation without a loss of face, so I said: 'Hey, I'm going to your class. Wanna walk with me there?' And he got up and walked with me."

Sooner or later, empaths get used to being comfortable with being uncomfortable. Assert your truth and make changes for your own benefit when you feel inclined to spend time elsewhere, without feeling responsible for others' positions. It may also be true that conditions may shift once you declare your exit plan, as change often brings clarity for more than just one person. By taking good care of yourself, you may inspire positive outcomes for many.

Ultimately, individuals have to decide for themselves where they can best live, and serve, and exercise their own beliefs and convictions.

Love Is Everywhere

To re-align with an empathic sense of harmony (with a sense of gratitude) and prepare yourself to step out into the world, try this meditation.

Spend a few moments in one location, looking at the structure of the place itself. If it is a room, notice the ceilings, the floors. Are there windows? Look for the door or entrance. As you breathe in deeply, notice any furniture that may be there surrounding you. Breathe it all in and exhale it all out. Then take a few moments to recognize the gift in each object, as well as in the room itself—including the air that fills it. Going one by one, say: "You love me. I love you." For example:

"Ceiling, I love you and you love me. Thank you for protecting me."

"Windows, you love me and I love you. Thank you for giving me a viewpoint."

"Floor, I love you and I know you love me. Thank you for supporting my weight as I come and go."

You can also add genuine personal sentiments like:

"Wall, I love you and you love me. Thank you for giving me a way to enclose myself, for giving me privacy and safety. Although you are stucco, which is not my favorite, I love you anyway."

Remember: playfulness is key!

These conversations can continue outside as well. That tree out front may appreciate your embrace. The buds and clover may sway with the sighs of admiration you emit. The air you breathe, the clouds coasting above you—imagine loving them all with consciousness. Imagine them all loving you and shining their inner light your way. Even what you may suppose to be only a dumb rock, or a clump of dirt. Engage with all of it with a sense of wonderment and heartfelt gratitude.

As you encounter or see people, notice how they move about, perhaps under a great arching tree bough, never aware of how their surroundings set the most lovely stage for them as they pass by. Kindly observe the counter clerk who is often under some pressure and subject to scrutiny from eager eyes. Imagine each cell of both your beings lit up with life, with a bright spark of stardust. Watch people scurry, impatient to get wherever they need to go, with their cares etched on their faces. Think of them with love; send love out to them from your heart.

Silent benevolence has a great impact on the giver and most likely upon the receiver as well. Let there be a resonance radiating from you to anyone you encounter, anyone you think of, even those who trouble you. Think of each thought as a leaf blowing in the wind of time, a reminder of the passing nature of the form you now have, but with the eternal light of your soul and theirs beaming out into the world as a gift of unique vibrancy. Attune to a loving rapport, to a spiritual and embracing harmony between yourself and everything and everyone with whom you come into contact on any given day.

Make it be so!

Conclusion: Heal the World

We live in an increasingly polarized world. We can contact people across the globe, but we are fragmented. We can communicate with total strangers on the internet but may not be on speaking terms with our own family members or neighbors. The extremes in our viewpoints make the space between us a battle ground, an agitated area where anything but positive connection is possible.

When communication fails and polarization is the norm, society becomes like a broken bridge. Empaths can keep creating ways to infuse the world with compassion by bringing a spiritual, creative energy to generate positive feelings in others and to encourage healing where wounds are fresh from constant verbal slashing. But if no one is listening, their efforts are futile. We are only alive for a brief time. And whatever points we feel we need to score in our increasingly conflicted and isolating world are not really the point at all. Our love for one another is the point. When benevolence unravels, shredding the empathic threads that connect us, we all suffer. We all become desensitized and destructive.

So how can empaths survive in this world? To be empathic is to be open to understanding why others feel they must act (or why they choose to act) in certain ways, without being responsible for them or their choices. This open-heartedness—this seeking to feel and then better understand others—has in it the potential to reach what ancient Jewish scholars and mystics described as our mission in life—*tikkun olam*, to heal the world.

For empaths, the meaning of life lies in feeling deeply and negotiating their intuitive sensing by attempting to understand. This comes naturally to them. True empathy and empathic knowing never seeks to criticize destructively. It takes many years to come fully into a genuinely empathic presence, because it is so easy to skip over the first crucial step of making a dedicated commitment to understanding others. Empathic knowing requires that we look at people and imagine them as worthy, unique beings. It isn't driven by a need or desire to control or to criticize. It grows rather from a curiosity about how others came to be as they are.

This is the time for empathic people to have courage, to be unafraid to dwell on thoughts of healing, to express visions of wholeness, and to create that which will transform discord into harmony. If empaths don't do it, who will?

ACKNOWLEDGMENTS

I'd like to thank my agent, Lisa Hagan, for her guidance, wisdom, and empathic sisterhood. I'd also like to thank the many people who shared their accounts of their lives as empaths with me and allowed me to include them in this book. And finally, I thank my friend and cousin, Christie Hunt Suppan, for her enduringly empathic presence in my life.

ABOUT THE AUTHOR

 Elaine Clayton has been a published author for over thirty years. Her work includes illustrations for Pulitzer Prize-winning author Jane Smiley and for Gregory Maguire, author of the novel that inspired the popular Broadway musical *Wicked*. Her books for adults on intuitive intelligence include *Making Marks: Discover the Art of Intuitive Drawing*.

Elaine lives in Connecticut and Georgia with her family, where she works in her studio and is the mother of two sons and a pug named Miss Georgia. She is a Reiki master and teacher. To learn more about her books for children and other art, portraits, and murals, visit *elaineclayton.com*

HAMPTON ROADS
PUBLISHING
COMPANY

. . . for the evolving human spirit

Hampton Roads Publishing Company publishes books on a variety of subjects, including spirituality, health, and other related topics.

For a copy of our latest trade catalog, call (978) 465-0504 or visit our distributor's website at *www.redwheelweiser.com*. You can also sign up for our newsletter and special offers by going to *www.redwheelweiser.com/newsletter/.net*